SUPERCHARGED STORYTIMES

Supercharged

STORYTIMES

An Early Literacy Planning and Assessment Guide

KATHLEEN CAMPANA / J. ELIZABETH MILLS / SAROJ NADKARNI GHOTING

ala editions

An imprint of the American Library Association
Chicago   2016

KATHLEEN CAMPANA is a doctoral candidate at the University of Washington Information School. She has a background in school and corporate libraries. Her research focuses on the learning that occurs for children and youth in library programs and the role that family engagement plays in that learning. She has served as a research assistant on the VIEWS2 research grant for all four years.

J. ELIZABETH MILLS is a doctoral student and a MLIS graduate from the University of Washington Information School. She has a background in children's literature as an editor and author. She studies how librarians are planning and presenting their storytimes in terms of learning theory and interactivity with respect to technology in storytimes. She has been a research assistant on the grant for three years.

SAROJ NADKARNI GHOTING is an Early Childhood Literacy Consultant and national trainer on early literacy. She presents early literacy training and information sessions at national, regional, and state conferences, and training for library staff and their partners. She has been a consultant for the Public Library Association and the Association for Library Service to Children of the American Library Association on the Every Child Ready to Read @ your library early literacy initiative and coauthor of four other books on early literacy and storytimes.

© 2016 by Kathleen Campana, J. Elizabeth Mills, and Saroj Nadkarni Ghoting

Extensive effort has gone into ensuring the reliability of the information in this book; however, the publisher makes no warranty, express or implied, with respect to the material contained herein.

ISBN: 978-0-8389-1380-2 (paper)

Library of Congress Cataloging-in-Publication Data

Names: Campana, Kathleen, author. | Mills, J. Elizabeth, author. | Ghoting, Saroj Nadkarni, author.
Title: Supercharged storytimes : an early literacy planning and assessment guide / Kathleen Campana, J. Elizabeth Mills, Saroj Nadkarni Ghoting.
Description: Chicago : ALA Editions, an imprint of the American Library Association, 2016. | Includes bibliographical references and index.
Identifiers: LCCN 2015043424 | ISBN 9780838913802 (paper)
Subjects: LCSH: Children's libraries—Activity programs. | Children's libraries—Activity programs—Evaluation. | Language arts (Early childhood)—Activity programs. | Language arts (Early childhood)—Activity programs—Evaluation. | Project VIEWS2. | Children's libraries—Activity programs—United States—Case studies. | Storytelling.
Classification: LCC Z718.3 .C36 2016 | DDC 027.62/51—dc23 LC record available at http://lccn.loc .gov/2015043424

Cover design by Kimberly Thornton. Imagery © Shutterstock, Inc.
Text design by Alejandra Diaz in the Cordale, Gotham and Phoreus Cherokee typefaces.

♾ This paper meets the requirements of ANSI/NISO Z39.48–1992 (Permanence of Paper).
Printed in the United States of America

20 19 18 17 16   5 4 3 2 1

We dedicate this book to Dr. Eliza T. Dresang; to the librarians who were part of the study; and to everyone who helped shepherd this work into the light. Storytimes Matter!

—KC and JEM

■ ■ ■

And to all library staff who continually reflect on how best to serve children, their families, and their caregivers. Hooray!

—SNG

CONTENTS

Foreword by Diane Hutchins, Early Learning Consultant, Washington State Library   ix
Acknowledgments   *xiii*
Read Me First!   *xv*

PART I
A COMMITMENT TO EARLY LITERACY IN STORYTIMES   **1**

■ **Project VIEWS2: The Storytime Study**   3

1   Supercharged Storytimes and the VIEWS2 Planning Tool   5

PART II
HOW TO SUPERCHARGE YOUR STORYTIME!   **15**

■ **The Relationship between VIEWS2 and ECRR**   17

■ **VIEWS2 Planning Tool (VPT)**   21

2   Talking   31

3   Reading   45

4   Singing   61

5   Playing   75

6   Writing   89

PART III

ASSESSING YOUR SUPERCHARGED STORYTIME — **105**

■ **Project VIEWS2: Exploring Storytime Assessment** — 107

7 Self-Reflection — 111

8 Peer Mentoring in the Field — 117

9 The Big Picture: Incorporating Assessment in Your Storytime Practice — 125

PART IV

THE FUTURE OF EARLY LEARNING AND STORYTIMES — **133**

■ **Moving beyond VIEWS2** — 135

10 Before You Go — 137

Appendix A   *Storytime Assessment Worksheets*   *141*
Appendix B   *VIEWS2/Head Start Early Learning Outcomes Crosswalk*   *151*
Appendix C   *VPT Organized by Age*   *155*

VIEWS2 Glossary of Terms   *163*
Index   *165*

FOREWORD

DO PUBLIC LIBRARY STORYTIMES MAKE A DIFFERENCE? THIS IS A challenging question. Do children really benefit in a practical way from public library storytime programs? Although library staff who interact with children at early literacy programs may sense that they do benefit, is there any evidence that these programs actually help children learn to read? Is it even possible to create valid and reliable instruments that can measure the effectiveness of public library storytimes?

WHY IS THIS IMPORTANT?

Libraries matter—or do they? In 1998, Washington's public libraries had asked to be part of a statewide discussion on early learning, but were turned away. That denial was a wake-up call that inspired the libraries to join forces, eventually leading to the creation of the Early Learning Public Library Partnership (ELPLP). Leaders in Washington's public library community soon realized that telling funders and decision makers, "Libraries matter," was no longer enough. Libraries needed to be able to demonstrate that their programs really do make a difference and that funding public libraries is a wise investment. Directors of public libraries throughout the state of Washington were starting to ask researchers at every opportunity: "How can we show that the early literacy focus of storytimes makes a difference in the ability of children to learn how to read successfully?"

In 2009, the iSchool of the University of Washington was awarded the first of two successive National Leadership Grants by the Institute for Museum and Library Services (IMLS) for Project VIEWS (Valuable Initiatives in Early Learning that Work Successfully), the first study to assess the impact of early literacy storytimes in public libraries. The Washington State Library (WSL), believing in the value of such a research project, allocated a portion of its Library Services and Technology Act (LSTA) grants to the state's funds to help support the work of Project VIEWS. Thrive Washington, a public-private partnership that coordinates the work of the ELPLP, also partnered with the iSchool on what was to be a truly unique project. Ultimately, Project VIEWS was successful in providing a way for Washington's public libraries to demonstrate their value as community early learning partners.

IT TOOK A VILLAGE OF EXTRAORDINARY PEOPLE

As project manager of Connecting the Dots, the WSL project that helped to support VIEWS and VIEWS2, I had the great privilege to work with the late Dr. Eliza T. Dresang, the principal investigator for both Project VIEWS and Connecting the Dots. I was also fortunate to have known and collaborated with many of the talented researchers, representing multiple disciplines, who worked with her on this groundbreaking study. At the advisory meeting that was held after the VIEWS2 field observations were completed, I was surrounded by a roomful of passionate, creative staff who had been randomly selected from the ELPLP membership to have their storytimes observed and filmed as part of the study. There was no mistaking the contagious energy in the room. It inspired me to refer to their work as "Supercharged Storytimes." The name caught on—quite understandably so.

Shortly before Dr. Dresang's death, OCLC WebJunction asked her about the possibility of providing an introduction to the tools and techniques of Project VIEWS2 using the WebJunction online platform. As with all things related to Project VIEWS2, a collegial group of partners worked together to design the program and deliver it. The name of this program? "Supercharged Storytimes," of course! After a successful launch in Washington State, Supercharged Storytimes expanded to five additional partner states in the fall of 2015. The ultimate goal is national implementation.

ELEVATING THE PROFESSION

Ask yourself the following questions:

- Are librarians who provide early literacy programs in public libraries considered "early learning professionals" by external organizations in your city, county, region, or state?
- Do public libraries even register in the minds of your local external early learning organizations when the topic of early learning comes up?
- Are librarians truly early learning professionals?

One of the most exciting aspects of Project VIEWS2 is its enormous potential to elevate the profession of librarianship (and by extension, museums and other informal early learning programs). By linking behaviors observed in library programs to the indicators of Washington State's Early Learning and Development Benchmarks, Project VIEWS2 has paved the way to make the connection between other specific, measurable library activities and educational benchmarks such as the Head Start Early Learning Outcomes Framework and Common Core standards; by demonstrating the ability of library staff to positively influence children's learning behaviors (as defined by state agencies dedicated to education), libraries may be seen as equal partners in the education of children and as legitimate early learning professionals.

TOGETHER IS BETTER

Partnering strengthened the ability of public libraries to fully participate in the advancement of early learning in Washington. Collaboration of effort in the early learning community—from planning to funding—made Project VIEWS2 a fantastic success.

Let this work inspire you. Experience the power of partnerships. See where the excitement of Supercharged Storytimes takes you!

—DIANE HUTCHINS
CONSULTANT/PROJECT MANAGER LIBRARY DEVELOPMENT
WASHINGTON STATE LIBRARY

ACKNOWLEDGMENTS

IT TAKES A VILLAGE TO DO MEANINGFUL RESEARCH AND WRITE A book about it, and we have benefited from an incredibly giving, collaborative, dedicated, and resourceful village.

First and foremost, we would like to acknowledge and honor Dr. Eliza T. Dresang—teacher, researcher, scholar, mentor, friend. Her vision of a study that could support and inform the work that children's librarians do every day through literacy-infused planning and evaluation tools resulted in Project VIEWS2, and this book is our humble attempt to put that research into practice.

We would like to thank the librarians and administrators who gave so much of their time to the study and to this book through interviews; many, many phone calls for guidance and support; and reading drafts. We could not have done any of this without you, and we are so grateful. Thank you for all that you do!

Our partners in this research provided both financial and community support throughout this incredible journey. Thank you to the Institute of Museum and Library Services, the University of Washington Information School, Thrive Washington, the Early Learning Public Library Partnership, and the Washington State Library. We especially thank Diane Hutchins at the Washington State Library, who coined the title of this book, wrote the foreword, and has been our tireless champion and torchbearer for the translation of research into practice We would also like to acknowledge the contributions of the rest of the research team: Dr. Janet Capps, Dr. Kathy Burnett, Dr. Erika Feldman, Dr. Bowie Kotrla, Marin Brouwer, Sean Fullerton, and Ivette Bayo Urban. Thank you to Dr. Cheryl Metoyer and Dr. Allyson Carlyle, our intrepid principal investigator and co-investigator following Dr. Dresang's passing. We are so grateful for your willingness to take on this study and mentor us through this process.

Thank you to our strategic advisory board, which steered the study so expertly throughout all four years.

We also thank the team at OCLC—Liz Morris, Betha Gutsche, and Kathleen Gesinger—for their excellent work in developing and implementing "Supercharged Storytimes," the introduction of this research to practitioners around the country.

Thank you, too, to our editor Jamie Santoro, who immediately understood our vision and encouraged us all along the way.

Finally, we would like to thank you, our readers, for your work with young children. We are all working toward making this a better world for them and helping them achieve in this world. We hope you will share your thoughts and stories with us.

◗ This research was made possible in part by the Institute of Museum and Library Services.

For additional information, visit the VIEWS2 website at http://views2.ischool.uw.edu.

READ ME FIRST!

THIS BOOK IS DESIGNED TO BE A GUIDE FOR YOU AND YOUR PRAC-
tice. However, it by no means represents the upper limit of what you can do to
supercharge your storytimes. Rather, the tools and tips in this book represent a
research-based approach that you can then infuse with your own creativity, imagination, and deep knowledge of your community. You do amazing work, and you
know your audience best. We hope to make your job easier by helping you to be
more intentional and advocate for what you do.

Based on the research of Project VIEWS2, we are offering some effective practices
to enhance your storytimes with early literacy behaviors that have been demonstrated to impact children's early literacy outcomes.

INTENTIONALITY, INTERACTIVITY, AND COMMUNITY

These three words carry such weight in summing up the most important pieces of
this research.

- When you are *intentional* about including specific early literacy behaviors in
  your storytime, you are impacting the children who attend. In addition, by
  intentionally articulating early literacy connections to caregivers, you are
  helping to support children's early literacy development.
- When you are *interactive* in the delivery of your storytime, you are demonstrating to children and caregivers alike that reading and learning are integral
  parts of a shared, enjoyable experience.
- When you rely on and learn from your peers, you are building a *community*
  that will help you continue to improve and hone your practice.

THIS BOOK FEATURES FOUR PARTS

Part I is an introduction to the VIEWS2 research and Supercharged Storytimes.

- Chapter 1 presents the main principles of Supercharged Storytimes and
  introduces the VIEWS2 Planning Tool (VPT).

Part II is an examination and exploration into how the VIEWS2 Planning Tool (VPT) fits into and supports the practices of Every Child Ready to Read at your library, 2nd edition (ECRR2). This is done through five chapters, each one looking at an ECRR2 practice in depth. Each chapter discusses the importance of that practice and ways that it can support early literacy.

- Chapter 2: Talking
- Chapter 3: Reading
- Chapter 4: Singing
- Chapter 5: Playing
- Chapter 6: Writing

Throughout these chapters, you will find sidebars with information and insights from library staff just like you whom we interviewed just for this book. We're calling them our experts, and it's true, they are! The sidebars offer tips and tricks for talking to parents, addressing large groups, scaffolding, and more. Though we don't specifically cover mixed-age storytimes, we do discuss each age group within each domain so you can draw on that information to help you plan for and respond to multiple ages in your storytime. At the end of each chapter, you'll find worksheets to guide you through a reflection of your storytimes with respect to the practices. In addition to information from our experts, you will see some quotes from VIEWS2 participants discussing their storytime practices.

You may notice as you go through each practice chapter that some of the early literacy behaviors and practices overlap. You are right! These activities do indeed support different aspects of early literacy. For example, there are similarities between talking and singing, especially with respect to domains such as alphabetic knowledge and phonological awareness. You can look at this overlap as confirmation that what you do touches on so many aspects of early literacy development; use this to advocate for the importance of your work in the lives of the children who attend your storytimes.

TITLES

Across the country, individuals providing library storytimes carry many titles, such as librarian, storytime provider or presenter, and storyteller. These titles may be based on job description, education, or a myriad of other things. The result is that there is not one universal term to use when referring to individuals who provide storytimes. Therefore, for the purposes of this book, we had to make an intentional decision as to which term to use. You will see in the following pages that we chose to use a combination of *librarian* and *storytime provider*. We recognize that many of you prefer the term *storytime provider* or *presenter*. However, we chose to continue to use the term *librarian* in specific cases.

- *Librarian* is used to refer to the participants in the VIEWS2 research. These individuals were referred to as the VIEWS2 librarians from day one and many now self-identify as a VIEWS2 librarian. In addition, we kept the term *librarian* intact in the quotes from our interviewees, as we did not want to change the content of their quotes.
- *Storytime provider* is used in all other content in the following pages.

We hope that you will understand that in most places, regardless of the term we use, we are addressing and referring to all of you who provide library storytimes.

Part III presents the findings of the last year of the Project VIEWS2 study, focusing on storytime assessment. We explore various types of assessment as well as their benefits and challenges; we look in depth at three library systems and their approaches to assessment; and we present recommendations based on our findings.

- Chapter 7 explores self-reflection as the most inward and personal method of assessment, one you can do every day and every time you offer storytimes.
- Chapter 8 explores peer mentoring as an assessment method that will more likely be used intermittently, perhaps even just a few times a year. We examine three case studies of ways in which library systems have implemented peer-mentoring methods that suit their needs.
- Chapter 9 explores how self-reflection and peer-mentoring fit together in an outcome-based assessment model that can help you develop an assessment program in your own practice. Our experts offer their recommendations about what to keep in mind when developing an assessment program, and we also discuss the importance of community.

Part IV covers next steps for research and practice, especially the community of practice orientations.

- Chapter 10 offers some final thoughts as you go forward to supercharge your storytimes.

Lastly, the appendices offer the VIEWS2 Planning Tool (VPT); self-reflection and peer-mentoring worksheets; and a crosswalk between the VIEWS2 Planning Tool and the Head Start Early Learning Outcomes Framework. The VPT language is based on the Washington State Early Learning Benchmarks. You can use the VPT to relate to your own state's early learning guidelines for language and literacy. The VIEWS2/Head Start crosswalk will help you understand how the VPT aligns with national benchmarks, and, in turn, will shed some light on how you can align the VPT with your state's early learning guidelines.

   We hope you enjoy this planning and assessment guide to supercharging your storytimes the VIEWS2 way!

A COMMITMENT TO EARLY LITERACY IN STORYTIMES

It is so exciting to be a part of the cutting edge of research that empowers librarians to be the leaders in early childhood literacy that we have always been, but now with the authority that gives us confidence and enthusiasm to do what we need to do, with focus and intent, to make a big difference in early literacy and lifelong learning for our youngest patrons.

—Gailene Hooper, Senior Librarian, NCRL Republic Branch

PROJECT VIEWS2
The Storytime Study

PROJECT VIEWS2 WAS A FOUR-YEAR STUDY FUNDED BY AN IMLS grant. During the first two years, we sought to understand whether the early literacy focus of public library storytimes is making a difference with the children who attend.

RESEARCH DESIGN

- Researchers used two tools (that together provide the foundation for the VIEWS2 Planning Tool, or VPT) to observe storytimes in forty libraries—including fourteen small, thirteen medium, and thirteen large libraries.
- One librarian from each of the forty libraries participated in the study.
- Three storytimes were observed in each library in each year.
- A total of 240 storytime observations were conducted in the forty libraries over two years.

Year 1

- Storytime were observed to establish what types of early literacy content and behaviors are occurring in storytimes.

Year 2

- Twenty of the librarians completed the VIEWS2 training, using the VPT to be more *intentional* with planning and reflecting on their early literacy content. The training accomplished this by providing librarians with:

  - the VPT, which offers early literacy behaviors they can use to encourage early literacy skills in children;
  - a more in-depth understanding of how their early literacy content maps to the early literacy skills so they can explain to parents why they are doing what they are doing in storytime;

- training and information on how to make their storytime practices more *interactive*;
- a *community* of practice made up of their peers to share ideas and gain feedback on what works and what does not; and
- information and support to help them reflect on the content of their storytime in order to grow and develop more effective storytime practices.

- Subsequent storytimes were observed to see if using the VPT to be more intentional in planning made a difference in early literacy storytime content and the children's early literacy behaviors.

THE FINDINGS

Year 1 established that:

- The librarians are including a wide variety of early literacy content in their storytimes.
- The children are demonstrating a wide variety of early literacy behaviors when attending storytimes.
- The children are responding to the early literacy content that librarians are including, with corresponding early literacy behaviors.

Year 2 established that:

- Training librarians on the principles included in the VIEWS2 training led to increased early literacy storytime content as well as increased early literacy behaviors from the children attending those storytimes.

> ❯ For additional information, visit the VIEWS2 website at http://views2.ischool.uw.edu.

SUPERCHARGED STORYTIMES AND THE VIEWS2 PLANNING TOOL

EARLY LITERACY STORYTIMES ARE THE CORNERSTONE of children's programming at the public library. And yet, up till now, we have not known whether these storytimes were truly making a difference with the children who attend them. The Project VIEWS2 research demonstrates that children are in fact responding to the early literacy content that storytime providers include. Storytimes are indeed making a difference in children's early literacy behaviors at storytime!

Furthermore, the Project VIEWS2 research demonstrated that an intentional focus on early literacy content in public library storytimes can increase the children's early literacy behaviors while at storytime. This is momentous news for library storytime providers across the nation and should be used to advocate for and demonstrate the value of your storytimes.

So what does this mean for your storytimes and your storytime practices? Essentially it means that being more intentional about incorporating early literacy content into your storytimes makes a stronger impact on children's early literacy behaviors. Storytimes are full of early literacy opportunities. You are already doing a number of things that support early literacy. By inserting more early literacy content into your storytimes, you can supercharge your practice and take it to the next level.

WHAT IS EARLY LITERACY?

Early literacy is what children know about reading and writing before they can actually read and write. Or, to be more complete, you could use this definition: Early literacy is what children know about communication, language (verbal and nonverbal), reading, and writing before they can actually read and write. It encompasses all of a child's experiences with conversation, stories (oral and written), books, and print. Early literacy is *not* the teaching of reading. It refers to laying a strong foundation so that when children are taught to read, they are ready.

Luckily, supercharging your storytimes can be easier than you think. Being intentional about incorporating a variety of early literacy content can be done even without a lot of planning time. This guide will help you learn how to supercharge your storytime by inserting the early literacy behaviors from the VIEWS2 Planning Tool into your storytime activities using the five practices from Every Child Ready to Read 2nd Edition (ECRR2): talking, reading, singing, playing, and writing.[1] Using these practices in an interactive manner is crucial for incorporating early literacy skills in informal learning environments such as library storytimes.

THE OVERALL *HOWS* OF SUPERCHARGING YOUR STORYTIME

So, what *is* a supercharged storytime? It is one where you:

- intentionally support early literacy;
- fill it with interactive moments that allow the children to interact with the storytime content;
- find creative and fun ways to insert early literacy into all storytime content;
- are flexible in adapting to the children's needs; and
- articulate early literacy connections to parents/caregivers.

The supercharged approach, based on the VIEWS2 training that occurred as a part of the research study, is designed to encourage storytime providers to be intentional about including early literacy content in their storytimes. The name Supercharged Storytimes was adopted as the principles highlighted by the VIEWS2 training were transitioned into practice. Three main principles are emphasized when supercharging your storytime:

- **Intentionality**—being more intentional with including early literacy in your storytime planning and reflection as well as offering early literacy tips to caregivers as part of storytime
- **Interactivity**—providing a variety of ways for the children to interact with and participate in your storytime content
- **Community**—building a community of your peers to allow you to share and receive ideas and get feedback

In addition to these three main principles, the Supercharged Storytimes program also emphasizes scaffolding as a method for supporting children's learning and self-reflection as a method for supporting your own learning and growth in your storytime practices.

Intentionality

An intentional focus refers to being more proactive about incorporating early literacy content into your storytime planning and reflection. It involves identifying the specific skills that you want to encourage and being thoughtful about how you are encouraging them in storytime.

> While I was already doing some things to support early literacy, participating in the VIEWS2 training made me want to do that much more to reinforce the early learning skills and to think about it more as I plan my storytimes. So instead of just choosing my books and maybe doing one thing that would reinforce it, I might add three things that will reinforce skills.
>
> —**VIEWS2 participant**

An intentional focus does not stop with planning your storytime. Intentionality is also crucial to your storytime delivery, making sure you are deliberate in your interactions with the children and their parents/caregivers during storytime in order to best support their learning. Finally, intentionality also includes reflecting on your storytime to understand its impact as well as successes and challenges.

The VIEWS2 Planning Tool (VPT) supports this intentional focus by providing a framework that helps you:

- understand the behaviors you can use to encourage specific early literacy skills;
- recognize when the children are responding to the early literacy content you are including; and
- provide additional behaviors to support and scaffold children's early literacy development.

This intentional approach enables you to be more specific and deliberate about the types of early literacy skills that you include in your storytimes and the ways in which you include them. By intentionally planning and reflecting on the early literacy content in your storytimes, you will be able to constantly tweak your storytimes to better serve the early literacy needs of the children who attend, thereby making a stronger impact in your community.

Interactivity

The VIEWS2 training hinges on and centers around the key concept of *interactivity*. Interactivity is the most important research-based "how" of inserting early literacy into storytimes.

By *interactivity*, we mean that the storytime provider incorporates elements during which the child can interact with the content of the storytime. It is about having a dialogue with the children, a back-and-forth exchange around the storytime content. Most important, you want to give the children time and opportunities to respond.

> One very important thing is to make sure that you give the children time to respond. That may seem like a self-evident thing, but I wasn't really giving them enough time to think about my questions and respond before I might answer for myself and move on.
>
> —**VIEWS2 participant**

> Whenever I can, I have the children help me tell the story. It improves a lot of their early literacy skills— their narrative skills, their vocabulary—and we are trying to build those skills before they start school.
>
> —Erica Delavan, Children's Librarian, Seattle Public Library

This is a change from the traditional storytime model of a one-way performance for the children. Interactive storytimes have gained importance because we now understand that, for young children, learning mostly occurs in the interactions they have with adults. Interactivity serves as the umbrella technique, or the overall *how*, to incorporate and model talking, reading, singing, playing, and writing (the five ECRR2 practices)[2] in order to supercharge your storytimes.

Some methods for encouraging interactivity are:

- Having the children act out something that is happening in the book, song, or rhyme
- Asking the children questions about the book and pausing so that they have a chance to respond
- Asking children to repeat or fill in words in a book, song, or rhyme

Being interactive with your storytime children allows you to shape the early literacy concepts that you are sharing with them through books, songs, rhymes, flannelboard activities, and other storytime elements. We want to emphasize that you can incorporate interactive elements throughout and in all of your storytime practices. Most important, interactivity allows you to identify where the children are developmentally so that you can support and encourage them to reach the next level in early literacy skills.

Scaffolding

One way that you can support children in their early literacy learning as they progress to the next level is *scaffolding*. To understand scaffolding, think of climbing up a ladder to the top of a construction-site scaffold. It means adding on a little bit to what a child is demonstrating that they already know. Scaffolding is essentially taking the broader skill that you want to encourage and breaking it into smaller portions, with each portion being a little more difficult until the child has mastered the skill. When an adult scaffolds information for a child, the child can interact with the information in smaller, more manageable pieces. According to Gray and MacBlain, "In practice, scaffolding is happening everywhere around us. We see parents structuring activities for their children, older siblings structuring tasks for younger members of the family, and attentive grandparents patiently taking their young grandchild through sequences of activities, which they have broken down into small steps and which they explain carefully along the way."[2]

Scaffolding is incredibly important to a child's learning process. Research in children's museums has shown that children will stay at museum exhibits longer and learn more when an accompanying adult is actively involved in scaffolding their learning process.[3] You can use scaffolding to move early learners beyond their current developmental stage or skills set and into progressively more difficult tasks. Scaffolding involves you and the other adults and children in the storytime providing support and modeling strategies for the child or other children in the storytime. Scaffolding also helps children build on information they may have already learned to extend their knowledge.

Repetition plays a significant role in scaffolding. As you repeat activities from week to week, children will begin to master the skills included in the activities, which then allows you to include new skills in the activities. Think of the age groups in the VPT as the children's developmental stages. Say your storytime is for children ages 18 to 36 months. Consider looking at the behaviors for children who are 36 to 60 months and incorporating those into your storytime activities if you notice your children have mastered the level for their age group. Exposure to different techniques will help their overall early literacy development.

Storytime Provider Community

Another important piece to developing supercharged storytimes is to find a group of fellow storytime providers (or even one other storytime provider) who are just as excited as you are about taking storytimes to the next level. See if they want to work through this guide with you. Working with peers to develop early literacy storytimes will give you a community with whom you can share and receive activity ideas; get support, advice, or feedback; and ask questions. Try to meet regularly in person, over Skype, or via conference call to support each other. If you cannot meet very often, use e-mail or social media to stay connected to your community. This emphasis on community was incorporated into the Project VIEWS2 training and the storytime providers felt that being able to share with their colleagues and ask questions was incredibly helpful in supercharging their practice.

> [The community] helped me to feel connected, like I don't have to reinvent the wheel. There are others out there that are doing this, too, and I don't have to be perfect at it, but every little bit helps—also knowing that there are others that are also working through what's going to work and what's not going to work.
>
> — VIEWS2 participant

Self-Reflection

A final important piece to supercharging your storytime is finding ways to reflect on your storytime and get feedback on it. Self-reflection and peer mentoring (peer coaching) will become important to you as a storytime provider because both techniques can help you grow and improve. As a children's storytime provider you have the freedom and creativity to plan, adapt, and change your storytimes. You are not held to a curriculum. Because of this flexibility, you constantly need to reflect on your storytime content as well as how the children (and parents/caregivers) respond to it in order to understand whether your activities are impactful. Peer mentoring based on storytime observations can also be a powerful feedback method for you to use. Because of their experience observing your storytime, your peers will be able to give you positive and constructive feedback on your content as well as how the children responded. The final section in this book will dive deeper into self-reflection and peer mentoring.

It's not something that turns storytime into dull boring lessons. The lessons and techniques are really invisible, but they are something that librarians naturally do and parents naturally do. When they know to emphasize [storytime] and know to emphasize certain techniques in reading to their children, then the research shows that children do succeed.

—Dr. Eliza T. Dresang

Now that you know the big picture of Supercharged Storytimes, let's take a look at the VIEWS2 Planning Tool and how you use it.

WHAT IS THE VIEWS2 PLANNING TOOL?

The VIEWS2 Planning Tool (VPT) evolved from the research to help you be more intentional in including early literacy elements in your storytime in interactive ways. Early literacy can be broken down in different categories, as evidenced in the language and literacy divisions in the early learning guidelines for each state. VIEWS2 researchers used the 2005 Washington State Benchmarks.

VIEWS2 Early Literacy Domains

- **Communication**: the ability to vocalize, move, or speak in a way that other people can understand and respond to
- **Language Use**: the ability to communicate for a variety of purposes
- **Phonological Awareness**: the ability to recognize the sounds in words
- **Vocabulary**: children's development of a collection of words and language rules that are used and understood by others
- **Comprehension**: understanding what has been read or said
- **Print Concepts**: understanding that written language has meaning and can provide information and pleasure
- **Alphabetic Knowledge**: the ability to name letters, distinguish letter shapes, and identify letter sounds
- **Writing Skills**: include demonstrating the understanding that written shapes and letters have meanings

For each of the above domains there is a chart of early literacy behaviors. Each chart addresses one or more of the seventeen goals across the eight domains. Below is the VPT for Phonological Awareness.

As you can see in this chart, each domain goal is divided into two columns. The first column lists behaviors that the storytime provider can do to support the goal. The second column lists the behaviors that children will exhibit with the goal. So, if you incorporate the behaviors in the first column into your storytime content, you should start to see the children at your storytimes exhibiting the behavior in the second column. You may notice in other domains that some behaviors in the first column for the storytime provider do not have a direct correlation to the children's behaviors in the second column. This means that if you do incorporate that behavior in your storytime, even though they do not have a corresponding explicit behavior, they still work to encourage the broader early literacy goal. In addition, there are behaviors not listed in the first column that can still support the early literacy goal. The VPT is a guide, not a comprehensive listing.

In addition, each domain is divided into three age ranges: birth to 18 months, 18 to 36 months, and 36 to 60 months. Whether you are presenting a storytime

> ❶ There are behaviors beyond what is listed in the VPT that can still support early literacy skills. The VPT is a guide, not a comprehensive listing.

for a particular age level or for a mixture of ages, this breakdown allows you to simply look down and find behaviors to insert. Each age range includes several behaviors that relate to early literacy concepts. Keep in mind: these age ranges are also a guide. If most of your group is toward the older end of the targeted age range, feel free to include behaviors from the next age range. For example, if you have an older group at baby storytime, you could use some behaviors from the 18 to 36 month group. To continue to solidify early literacy skills for the children, you can also borrow from the behaviors in the younger age group to use with the older children.

Figure 1.1

VIEWS2 Valuable Initiatives in Early Learning that Work Successfully

Phonological Awareness / Playing with Sounds

■ Birth to 18 Months
READING GOAL 66: Children demonstrate phonological awareness

Educator/Adult	Children
Reads to children from books with developmentally appropriate content, and pauses to provide them time to insert the sounds of familiar words	Vocalize familiar words when read to
Uses rhymes in stories, greetings, and directions	Recite last word of familiar rhymes, with assistance

■ 18 Months to 36 Months
READING GOAL 66: Children demonstrate phonological awareness

Educator/Adult	Children
Uses reading style (e.g., pauses, providing children time to respond) where children can say the last word of familiar rhymes/songs	Complete a familiar rhyme or fingerplay by providing the last word
Invites children to act out a variety of tempos or speeds of sounds (e.g., clapping hands rapidly and then slowly; speaking rapidly and then slowly)	Imitate tempo and speed of sound

■ 36 Months to 60 Months
READING GOAL 66: Children demonstrate phonological awareness

Educator/Adult	Children
Reinforces recognition of beginning word sounds (e.g., "*Book* begins with the *b* sound.")	Identify initial sound of words, with assistance
Encourages children to find multiple objects in a picture with the same beginning sound	Find objects in a picture with the same beginning sound, with assistance
Points out the differences between similar-sounding words (e.g., *three* and *tree*)	Differentiate between similar-sounding words

Adult component (PET) by E. Feldman, E. Dresang, K. Burnett, J. Capps, and K. Campana. Children's component (BCPAF) by E. Feldman.

SUPERCHARGING YOUR STORYTIME WITH THE VIEWS2 PLANNING TOOL

The VPT is designed to be used in a flexible manner for planning. VIEWS2 research starts with *your* storytime. There are no prescribed materials; there is no prescribed format, order, or "dosage" for your storytime.

You can begin the planning process by looking at your storytime plan and thinking about what you already do or will do in your storytime. Review the VPT for each domain. What specific domains and goals are you already incorporating? Is there something in the first column that you could easily include? Another way to plan is to review the VPT for all the early literacy domains. Is there any domain that you notice you rarely include in your storytimes? Consider ways you might include it. The VPT allows you to be flexible in the amount of specific behaviors to include in a storytime program. You can choose to incorporate one behavior, several behaviors from one goal, or behaviors from several goals. You can also decide how to include these behaviors—through presentation of a book, a rhyme or song, or an activity; whatever works best for your storytime children. You have the flexibility to tailor your programming to the children and families who attend your storytimes. Trust your own instincts and knowledge of your storytime community.

The important thing at the beginning is to start out slowly. You don't want to overwhelm yourself. Pick one or two behaviors and decide how to insert them in your storytime. Don't worry! The next section of the book explains this process using the five practices from ECRR2 mentioned above: talking, reading, singing, playing, and writing. You are probably already including some of the behaviors in your storytime activities; you just may have not been as intentional about inserting them, or you may have not been able to articulate to parents why you were using these behaviors. These tools will help you to be more intentional and to communicate the importance of what you are doing to parents and other stakeholders.

Work with these practices and behaviors until you feel comfortable with them and then try some different ones in the VPT. Again, there is no specific way to do this. There is no prescription or recipe. Trust that you are best able to build on your storytime experiences, knowledge, approach, and style based in part on knowing your own community. By the same token, be open to expand how you plan and present storytimes as you reflect on the VPT and the principles of Supercharged Storytimes: intentionality, interactivity, and community. These tools give you the flexibility to create a supercharged storytime, filled with early literacy content that benefits your storytime community.

An important benefit of the VPT is that it also gives you a way to talk with parents and caregivers about what you are doing. As you are doing an activity with the children, you are also modeling for the parents and caregivers, so take a moment to explain the importance of what you are doing and why you are doing it. Based on feedback from our VIEWS2 librarians, we also included some more approachable terms in the VPT that you can use to refer to the skills when talking to parents and caregivers. For example, while you are playing a rhyming game, you can mention to parents and caregivers that rhyming encourages playing with the sounds of words (or phonological awareness), which can later lead to understanding the sounds that letters make and then being able to read words. Essentially the VPT will help you link your storytime content to the early literacy skills. Each of the following chapters features tips from librarians on how they talk with parents and caregivers about a particular practice.

What we want you to take away from this book and from the VPT is that you can infuse early literacy learning into most anything you do in storytime, through all activities, and not just be tied to the reading of a book. The most important thing is to keep activities fun and interactive. If the children have a chance to interact with you, they will engage in and learn from whatever you are doing. Be intentional about including early literacy behaviors throughout all your storytimes. The VIEWS2 research demonstrated that the children are responding to the early literacy content that you are presenting, so being intentional about increasing your early literacy content in your storytimes is going to have a positive impact on the children that attend them.

Before we move into the nuts and bolts of how to supercharge your storytimes, we want to emphasize a few key points.

1. Most important, the library is an informal learning environment, so the learning process will be very different than in a formal learning environment. While an informal learning environment works to support the learning that is taking place in formal learning environments, informal learning environments are also supporting lifelong learning.
2. In order to support lifelong learning, it is important to demonstrate that learning can be fun and enjoyable, self-motivated, self-paced and a social experience. One of the most significant ways that you can support lifelong learning with young children is to show them that learning can be fun and enjoyable.
3. Along with this, we want to emphasize that your storytime can support all types of learning without turning them into lessons and classes. By being intentional, interactive, and fun, you can incorporate all types of learning into your typical storytime activities.

Bottom line: As you work through this book, strive to ensure that all your early literacy activities are interactive and fun!

NOTES

1. Public Library Association (PLA) and Association for Library Services to Children (ALSC), "Every Child Ready to Read @ Your Library—2nd Edition," 2011, www.everychildreadytoread .org.
2. Colette Gray and Sean MacBlain, Learning Theories in Childhood (Los Angeles: SAGE, 2012), 142.
3. Laurel Puchner, Robyn Rapoport, and Suzanne Gaskins, "Learning in Children's Museums: Is It Really Happening?", CURA Curator: The Museum Journal 44, no. 3 (2001): 237–59.

HOW TO SUPERCHARGE YOUR STORYTIME!

We believe in early learning, and in the inclusion of very deliberate pieces of early learning strategies to be incorporated into a storytime. We want to provide our families with strong models of ways to support their children. To do this, we make sure that the storytimes themselves—while they may include all these elements—continue to be not only developmentally appropriate but fun.

—Judy Nelson, Customer Experience Manager—Youth,
Pierce County (Washington) Library System

THE RELATIONSHIP BETWEEN VIEWS2 AND ECRR

YOU ARE PROBABLY ALREADY FAMILIAR WITH, AND MAY HAVE HAD training on ECRR1[1] and ECRR2.[2] ECRR1 laid out six early literacy skills, and ECRR2 presented the early literacy components and practices. The VIEWS2 Planning Tool (VPT) also has early literacy domains (defined below) that align with the skills and components from ECRR. While the early literacy domains in the VPT are broken down in a different way than the six skills of ECRR1 and the components of ECRR2, they all fit together naturally, as they are fundamentally referring to the same types of early literacy knowledge. Just as with your own state's early learning guidelines, you will find that the knowledge base of early literacy is the same. It is just configured in different ways.

Figure II.1 shows the relationship between the early literacy domains from VIEWS2, the early literacy skills from ECRR1, and the early literacy components from ECRR2. As we have discussed in the last section, it is crucial to infuse early literacy—whether it is the ECRR1 skills, the ECRR2 components, or the VPT domains—into the five practices from ECRR2. Because of this, in figure II.1, we have also included the ECRR2 practices that work best for encouraging specific types of early literacy domains.

EARLY LITERACY DOMAINS OF VIEWS2

- **Communication**: the ability to vocalize, move, or speak in a way that other people can understand and respond to
- **Language Use**: the ability to communicate for a variety of purposes
- **Phonological Awareness**: the ability to recognize the sounds in language
- **Vocabulary**: children's development of a collection of words and language rules that are used and understood by others
- **Comprehension**: understanding what has been read or said
- **Print Concepts**: understanding that written language has meaning and can provide information and pleasure
- **Alphabetic Knowledge**: the ability to name letters, distinguish letter shapes, and identify letter sounds
- **Writing Skills**: include demonstrating the understanding that written shapes and letters have meanings

Figure II.1

Crosswalk between VIEWS2 Planning Tool (VPT) and ECRR1 & 2

VPT Domains	ECRR1 Early Literacy Skills	ECRR2 Early Literacy Components	ECRR2 Early Literacy Practices	
• Comprehension	• Vocabulary • Narrative Skills	• Oral Language • Vocabulary • Background Knowledge	• Talking • Reading • Singing	• Playing • Writing
• Writing Skills	• Print Awareness • Letter Knowledge	• Print Conventions/Awareness • Letter Knowledge	• Writing	
• Vocabulary	• Vocabulary	• Vocabulary	• Talking • Reading • Singing	• Playing • Writing
• Print Concepts	• Print Motivation	• Background Knowledge (Print Motivation)	• Talking • Reading	• Writing
• Print Concepts	• Print Awareness	• Print Conventions / Awareness	• Talking • Reading	• Playing • Writing
• Phonological Awareness	• Phonological Awareness	• Phonological Awareness	• Talking • Reading	• Singing
• Alphabetic Knowledge	• Letter Knowledge	• Letter Knowledge	• Talking • Reading	• Singing • Writing
• Communication	• Narrative Skills	• Oral Language	• Talking • Reading	• Playing • Writing
• Language Use	• Narrative Skills	• Oral Language	• Talking • Reading	• Playing • Writing

EARLY LITERACY SKILLS OF ECRR1[3]

- **Vocabulary:** knowing the meanings of words
- **Print Motivation:** a child's interest in and enjoyment of books and reading
- **Print Awareness:** knowing that print has meaning; how to handle a book
- **Phonological Awareness:** the ability to hear and play with the smaller sounds in words
- **Letter Knowledge:** knowing that the same letter can look different, that letters have names and represent sounds
- **Narrative Skills:** the ability to recount stories and events

EARLY LITERACY COMPONENTS OF ECRR2[4]
(CRITICAL DIMENSIONS OF LANGUAGE AND LITERACY)

- **Oral Language:** speaking, listening and communication skills (includes narrative skills)
- **Phonological Awareness:** the ability to hear and play with the smaller sounds in words

- **Print Conventions**: understanding that print has meaning, that the printed word represents the words we speak; direction of text; how to handle a book
- **Letter Knowledge**: knowing that the same letter can look different, that letters have names and represent sounds
- **Vocabulary**: knowing the meanings of words, objects, actions, concepts, feelings, ideas
- **Background Knowledge**: prior knowledge—what a child knows about the world and how things work by the time they enter school; includes content knowledge, conceptual thinking, print motivation, and book and story knowledge

FIVE PRACTICES OF ECRR2

- Talking
- Singing
- Reading
- Writing
- Playing

Figure II.1 above shows how the VIEWS2 literacy domains relate to ECRR1 and ECRR2. So now you may be wondering where the VPT fits in. The VPT is another configuration of language and literacy skills, with articulated connections to children's developmental behaviors.

We see the VPT as sitting in between the VIEWS2 literacy domains (or the skills and components from ECRR1 and ECRR2) and the five practices of ECRR2. (See figure II.2.) The practices give you easy, concrete methods (talking, reading, singing, playing, and writing) to demonstrate for parents that they can use to encourage early literacy development with their children. The five practices are great for parents in that they represent easy, understandable ways to be an active participant in their child's learning. However, early literacy skills are important for storytime providers and library staff to understand what children need to learn to read. In addition to educating parents that they can play a role in their child's learning by talking, reading, singing, playing, and writing with their children, you also need to model *how* to do these things in order for them to have the most impact. This is where the VPT comes in. It is important to incorporate the early literacy behaviors from the VPT into the practices. In this way, you are modeling for parents how to make the most meaningful impact through these activities. In the following five chapters, we will explore how to incorporate the early literacy behaviors from the VPT into the five practices that you do in storytime.

> Your practice will be powerful and effective when, by using the VIEWS2 Planning Tool, you purposefully incorporate the early literacy skills from the VIEWS2 domains into the five practices of ECRR2.
>
> —VIEWS2 Research Team

Figure II.2

The Relationship between VIEWS2 and ECRR2 Practices

Ultimately, whether you are using the terms in ECRR1, ECRR2, or VIEWS2, the critical piece to remember is to intentionally "connect the dots" between what you do in storytimes to early literacy behaviors.

NOTES

1. Public Library Association (PLA) and Association for Library Services to Children (ALSC), 2004, "Every Child Ready to Read @ Your Library—1st Edition."

2. Public Library Association (PLA) and Association for Library Services to Children (ALSC), 2011, "Every Child Ready to Read @ Your Library—2nd Edition," www.everychildreadytoread.org.

3. PLA and ALSC, "Every Child Ready to Read—1st Edition."

4. PLA and ALSC, "Every Child Ready to Read—2nd Edition."

VIEWS2 PLANNING TOOL (VPT)

You can also find the VPT, as well as other resources, on our website:
http://views2.ischool.uw.edu/resources/

VIEWS2 Valuable Initiatives in Early Learning that Work Successfully

Communication/How to Talk and Share

■ Birth to 18 Months

ORAL AND WRITTEN COMMUNICATION GOAL 64: Children communicate effectively.

CONVENTIONS OF SOCIAL COMMUNICATION GOAL 65: Children understand and use the conventions of social communication.

Educator/Adult	Children
Provides pauses so that children can interject	Vocalize/use words and gestures to solicit attention
Encourages children to imitate simple words	Imitate words (e.g., simple greetings)
Greets children with nonverbal gestures (e.g., waves hello) in order to communicate	Uses nonverbal gestures for social conventions of greeting (e.g., waving goodbye)
Encourages caretakers to model eye contact and taking turns in communication as well as sounds and words one-on-one	Participates in a one-on-one conversation by making sounds or sometimes using words

■ 18 Months to 36 Months

ORAL AND WRITTEN COMMUNICATION GOAL 64: Children communicate effectively.

CONVENTIONS OF SOCIAL COMMUNICATION GOAL 65: Children understand social communication.

Educator/Adult	Children
Responds to children's use of appropriate cues to solicit attention	Address listener appropriately to get attention (e.g., when speaking to another child, using that child's name)
Prompts children to use adjectives to describe things or events in order to communicate effectively	Use adjectives to describe a thing or event (e.g., "big toy," "fun ride")
Provides children with the opportunity to use sound effects to convey meaning (e.g., "crash," "bang," "buzz," animal sounds)	Use sound effects in play
Provides children with the opportunity to participate in turn-taking conversations (e.g., "What did you like about the book?")	Begin to demonstrate taking turns in conversation

■ 36 months to 60 months

ORAL AND WRITTEN COMMUNICATION GOAL 64: Children communicate effectively.

CONVENTIONS OF SOCIAL COMMUNICATION GOAL 65: Children understand social communication.

Educator/Adult	Children
Solicits use of words, signs, or picture books to state points of view, likes/dislikes, and opinions; does not include questions with a "right" answer	State point of view, likes/dislikes, and opinions using words, signs, or picture books
Encourages children to pay attention through positive feedback	Pay attention to speaker during conversation
Points out facial expressions of characters in stories or encourages children to make their own facial expression to express emotions	Begin to demonstrate understanding of nonverbal cues (e.g., recognizing or making facial expressions for pride)

Adult component (PET) by E. Feldman, E. Dresang, K. Burnett, J. Capps, and K. Campana. Children's component (BCPAF) by E. Feldman.

Figure 1b

VIEWS2 Valuable Initiatives in Early Learning that Work Successfully

Language Use/How to Use Words

▪ Birth to 18 Months

EXPRESSIVE/ORAL LANGUAGE GOAL 62: Children use language for a variety of purposes.

Educator/Adult	Children
Provides or recites oral stories (e.g., nursery rhymes) to children in order to prompt them to express simple thoughts or ideas	Enjoy listening to oral stories
	Use single words to express thoughts and ideas (e.g., when seeing the sun, saying "sun")

▪ 18 Months to 36 Months

EXPRESSIVE/ORAL LANGUAGE GOAL 62: Children use language for a variety of purposes.

LISTENING GOAL 63: Children demonstrate an understanding of language by listening.

Educator/Adult	Children
Prompts children to recount events	Recount an event, with assistance
Prompts children to reflect on the sequence of events in an orally narrated story	Begin to follow the sequence of events in an orally narrated story
Provides opportunity for fingerplay (e.g., songs and games that use hand and finger gestures)	Enjoys fingerplay (i.e., songs and games that use hand and finger gestures)
Prompts children to point to objects within the pages of a book or within given context	Attempt to locate objects that are discussed by others

▪ 36 Months to 60 Months

EXPRESSIVE/ORAL LANGUAGE GOAL 62: Children use language for a variety of purposes.

LISTENING GOAL 63: Children demonstrate an understanding of language by listening.

Educator/Adult	Children
Asks questions about a recent event	Recount some details of a recent event
Encourages children to identify animals and invites personification (e.g., making animal sounds, moving like an animal)	Mimic animal sounds
Asks questions about specific details and events in a story and provides positive feedback when children recall details	Respond to questions with appropriate answers

Adult component (PET) by E. Feldman, E. Dresang, K. Burnett, J. Capps, and K. Campana. Children's component (BCPAF) by E. Feldman.

| Figure 1c | VIEWS2 Valuable Initiatives in Early Learning that Work Successfully |

Phonological Awareness / Playing with Sounds

■ Birth to 18 Months

READING GOAL 66: Children demonstrate phonological awareness

Educator/Adult	Children
Reads to children from books with developmentally appropriate content, and pauses to provide them time to insert the sounds of familiar words	Vocalize familiar words when read to
Uses rhymes in stories, greetings, and directions	Recite last word of familiar rhymes, with assistance

■ 18 Months to 36 Months

READING GOAL 66: Children demonstrate phonological awareness

Educator/Adult	Children
Uses reading style (e.g., pauses, providing children time to respond) where children can say the last word of familiar rhymes/songs	Complete a familiar rhyme or fingerplay by providing the last word
Invites children to act out a variety of tempos or speeds of sounds (e.g., clapping hands rapidly and then slowly; speaking rapidly and then slowly)	Imitate tempo and speed of sound

■ 36 Months to 60 Months

READING GOAL 66: Children demonstrate phonological awareness

Educator/Adult	Children
Reinforces recognition of beginning word sounds (e.g., "*Book* begins with the *b* sound.")	Identify initial sound of words, with assistance
Encourages children to find multiple objects in a picture with the same beginning sound	Find objects in a picture with the same beginning sound, with assistance
Points out the differences between similar-sounding words (e.g., *three* and *tree*)	Differentiate between similar-sounding words

Adult component (PET) by E. Feldman, E. Dresang, K. Burnett, J. Capps, and K. Campana. Children's component (BCPAF) by E. Feldman.

Figure 1d

VIEWS2 Valuable Initiatives in Early Learning that Work Successfully

Vocabulary / Understanding and Using Words

■ Birth to 18 Months

VOCABULARY GOAL 59: Children use expressive vocabulary.

GRAMMAR AND SYNTAX GOAL 60: Children demonstrate progression in grammar and syntax.

Educator/Adult	Children
Uses gestures in combination with words when communicating	Combine words and gestures (e.g., waving when saying goodbye)
Invites children to label familiar objects in books or in the environment	Uses eight to ten understandable words (e.g., *daddy*, *bottle*, *up*)
Presents children with the opportunity to label aspects of people, places, and events	Use short telegraphic sentences (e.g., "Me go" or "There Mama.")

■ 18 Months to 36 Months

VOCABULARY GOAL 59: Children use expressive vocabulary.

GRAMMAR AND SYNTAX GOAL 60: Children demonstrate progression in grammar and syntax.

Educator/Adult	Children
Introduces unfamiliar objects and prompts children to request labels from caregiver	Ask others to label unfamiliar objects
Uses simple three- to four-word sentences (with mostly one- to two-syllable words) at least twice, followed by a pause so children can imitate	Imitate simple two-word phrase/sentence
Provides experiences that prompt children to ask questions	Uses simple questions in speech, but may not use correct grammar
Invites children to use adjectives to describe objects or things described in stories	Uses adjectives in phrases (e.g., "big bag," "green bear")

■ 36 Months to 60 Months

VOCABULARY GOAL 59: Children use expressive vocabulary.

GRAMMAR AND SYNTAX GOAL 60: Children demonstrate progression in grammar and syntax.

Educator/Adult	Children
Models using multiple words to explain ideas (e.g., "Another way of saying that is . . .", defining a new concept/idea)	Uses multiple words to explain ideas (e.g., when talking about being mad, saying "angry," "frustrated," etc.)
Ask children to talk about how they feel about what is happening in the story	Uses words to express emotions (e.g., *happy*, *sad*, *tired*, *scared*)
Prompts children to share stories about/describe their preferences and previous experiences, then assists in putting in sequence (e.g., "Oh, you have also gone to a grocery store. What did you do when you got there first? Did you get a cart? What happened next?")	Describes a task, project, and/or event sequentially in three or more sentences

Adult component (PET) by E. Feldman, E. Dresang, K. Burnett, J. Capps, and K. Campana. Children's component (BCPAF) by E. Feldman.

Figure 1e

VIEWS2 Valuable Initiatives in Early Learning that Work Successfully

Comprehension / Understanding Words, Stories, Directions, Ideas, etc.

■ Birth to 18 Months

VOCABULARY GOAL 58: Children use receptive vocabulary.

COMPREHENSION GOAL 61: Children demonstrate comprehension and meaning in language.

Educator/Adult	Children
Uses simple words to give children single-step directions (e.g., "Please bring me the ball") or indirect invitations (e.g., "Let's listen") and provides time for them to respond (e.g., "Clap," children clap).	Respond appropriately to familiar words (e.g., "Clap," children clap)
	Follow single-step directions (e.g., bringing the ball when asked)
	Have a receptive vocabulary of more than fifty words in home language
Asks children simple questions that can be answered with gestures towards a particular person (e.g., "Where is Mommy?") or object; (e.g., "Where is your blanket?")	Point to familiar person(s) when requested
	Point to objects when named (e.g., pointing to blanket when asked, "Where is your blanket?")
Directs children's attention using visual gaze and/or gestures	Pay attention to what the speaker is looking at or pointing to

■ 18 Months to 36 Months

VOCABULARY GOAL 58: Children use receptive vocabulary.

COMPREHENSION GOAL 61: Children demonstrate comprehension and meaning in language.

Educator/Adult	Children
Prompts children to identify different body parts by pointing	Identify at least three body parts, when requested
Prompts children to identify people, objects or actions by name (e.g., "Who is this?" "What is this a picture of?" "What is this person doing?")	Identify some people, objects, and actions by name
Asks children simple questions (e.g., "Do you see birds in the trees around your house?") and pauses, allowing children time to respond	Answer simple questions with words or actions
Provides experiences that prompt children to ask questions or reflect some knowledge of events/phenomena	Ask questions that demonstrate knowledge of events or phenomena (e.g., "Why did the boy run away?" "How did the water turn blue?")

■ 36 Months to 60 Months

VOCABULARY GOAL 58: Children use receptive vocabulary.

COMPREHENSION GOAL 61: Children demonstrate comprehension and meaning in language.

Educator/Adult	Children
Contrasts real and made-up words to prompt children to talk about differences between words that are real and made up	Distinguish between real and made-up words
Asks questions that may elicit short verbal answers *or* gestures that demonstrate that children are following the story/activity/conversation	Respond to questions with verbal answers or gestures
Uses strategies to assist children in having a conversation by extending/expanding on thoughts or ideas expressed by others in regards to a story, book, or song (e.g., "I hear that you think the bunny is pretending the box is a car. Who else has an idea about what the bunny is doing? What type of car is it?")	Extend/expand on a thought or idea expressed by another
	Engage in conversation that develops a thought or idea (e.g., telling about a past event)

Adult component (PET) by E. Feldman, E. Dresang, K. Burnett, J. Capps, and K. Campana. Children's component (BCPAF) by E. Feldman.

VIEWS2 Valuable Initiatives in Early Learning that Work Successfully

Print Concepts / Connecting with Books and Stories

■ Birth to 18 Months

READING GOAL 68: Children demonstrate awareness of the print concepts.

READING GOAL 69: Children demonstrate comprehension of printed material.

READING GOAL 71: Children demonstrate appreciation and enjoyment of reading.

Educator/Adult	Children
Highlights and points to pictures or words in a book, spaces between words, or words representing pictured objects	Pay attention to pictures or words in books
Prompts children to point to pictures, characters, or objects in books	Point to familiar pictures, characters, and objects in books
Presents children with the opportunity to explore books (e.g., what is on the pages) as part of hands-on activity	Explore books (e.g., flipping or turning through pages)

■ 18 Months to 36 Months

READING GOAL 69: Children demonstrate comprehension of printed material.

READING GOAL 70: Children demonstrate awareness of written materials for a variety of purposes.

READING GOAL 71: Children demonstrate appreciation and enjoyment of reading.

Educator/Adult	Children
Prompts children to recall specific characters from age-appropriate stories	Recall specific characters or actions from familiar stories
Inserts pauses, providing children time to respond, and asks questions during story reading that allow children to make predictions	Anticipate what comes next in known stories, with assistance (e.g., predicting the next animal in an animal concept book)
Prompts children to respond to the emotional experiences or expressions of characters in books	Respond to emotional expressions in a book (e.g., pointing to a happy face)
Invites children to make comments on books read recently or in the past	Make comments on book

■ 36 Months to 60 Months

READING GOAL 68: Children demonstrate awareness of the print concepts.

READING GOAL 71: Children demonstrate appreciation and enjoyment of reading.

Educator/Adult	Children
Points to letters in the text and asks children to identify them	Identify some individual letters in text
Points out signs and symbols in the environment when reading picture books. Asks children if they've seen these before (e.g., "On your way to the library, did you stop at a light? Was it a red light like this one?")	Recognize some signs and symbols in the environment (e.g., stop sign or traffic light)
Asks children, "Do you have a favorite book? What's the title?"	Express the title of a favorite book

Adult component (PET) by E. Feldman, E. Dresang, K. Burnett, J. Capps, and K. Campana. Children's component (BCPAF) by E. Feldman.

VIEWS2 Valuable Initiatives in Early Learning that Work Successfully

Alphabetic Knowledge / Exploring with Letters

■ Birth to 18 Months

READING GOAL 67: Children demonstrate awareness of the alphabetic principle.

Educator/Adult	Children
Reads books with repetitive sounds and/or pronounces words deliberately and slowly when reading	Imitate sounds when looking at words in a book
Points toward a book while reading or when a book is within reach of children	Point to words in a book

■ 18 Months to 36Months

READING GOAL 67: Children demonstrate awareness of the alphabetic principle.

Educator/Adult	Children
Prompts children to recite or sing the letters of the alphabet	Recite a song with letters of the alphabet, with assistance (e.g., the alphabet song or a recitation)
Asks children to point to print on the page of a picture book or other illustrated page, poster, etc.	Begin to understand that print represents words (e.g., pretending to read text)

■ 36 Months to 60 Months

READING GOAL 67: Children demonstrate awareness of the alphabetic principle.

Educator/Adult	Children
Points out shapes with specific letters	Associate the names of letters with their shapes
Prompts children to match letters and sounds	Correctly identify ten or more letters of the alphabet
Prompts children to think about how letters and numbers are different	
Points to each word separately while reading	
Prompts children to identify the same word across pages of a book	

Adult component (PET) by E. Feldman, E. Dresang, K. Burnett, J. Capps, and K. Campana. Children's component (BCPAF) by E. Feldman.

VIEWS2 Valuable Initiatives in Early Learning that Work Successfully

Writing Concepts / Writing

■ Birth to 18 Months

WRITING GOAL 72: Children demonstrate alphabet knowledge.

WRITING GOAL 73: Children use writing skills and demonstrate knowledge of writing conventions.

WRITING GOAL 74: Children use writing for a variety of purposes.

Educator/Adult	Children
Asks children to point out words and pictures in a book in order to prompt children to think about the differences between words and pictures	Point to words in a book
	Imitate other person's writing, drawing, or scribbling by making their own marks or scribbles
Demonstrates making marks on a page in front of children	Scribble spontaneously

■ 18 Months to 36 Months

ORAL & WRITTEN COMMUNICATION GOAL 64: Children communicate effectively.

WRITING GOAL 72: Children demonstrate alphabet knowledge.

WRITING GOAL 74: Children use writing for a variety of purposes.

Educator/Adult	Children
Asks children about attempts to produce written, age-appropriate material (e.g., scribbles)	Scribble and make marks on paper purposefully
Uses hand to point out words as they are read	Demonstrate an understanding that we hear and see words by pointing randomly to text while it is being read out loud (i.e., that a spoken word is also represented in print)
Provides writing explorations related to fine motor skills, gross motor skills, and postural control	Draw horizontal and vertical lines

■ 36 Months to 60 Months

ORAL & WRITTEN COMMUNICATION GOAL 64: Children communicate effectively.

WRITING GOAL 72: Children demonstrate alphabet knowledge.

WRITING GOAL 73: Children use writing skills and demonstrate knowledge of writing conventions.

WRITING GOAL 74: Children use writing for a variety of purposes.

Educator/Adult	Children
Incorporates drawing into storytime activities	Begin to draw representational figures
Prompts children to find the same letter in different media (e.g., book, poster, sign)	Identify letters to match the said-aloud letter name
Provides activities that encourage drawing basic geometric shapes	Draw basic geometric shapes (e.g., circle, triangle)
Provides activities that encourage pretend writing	Use pretend writing activities during play to show print conventions in primary language
Invites children to make up and tell stories and write them out	Talk aloud about creative ideas and stories and ask adults to write them out
Invites children to work together to make up a poem and writes it out	Ask adults to write out rhymes to make a simple poem

Adult component (PET) by E. Feldman, E. Dresang, K. Burnett, J. Capps, and K. Campana. Children's component (BCPAF) by E. Feldman.

TALKING

~~~~~~

Talking is the most important thing I do, actually. I want kids to know that reading and having conversations about books and with adults and people in general isn't a one-sided thing. I also think it's important to learn turn taking and social skills, like when it's okay to talk and when it isn't. But in my storytimes it's always okay to talk.

—Sara Lachman, Youth Services Librarian, Olympia Timberland Library[1]

ALKING IS ONE OF THE MOST INTEGRAL PRACTICES TO storytimes. From the moment you welcome children at the door to the moment during craft time when you say, "Tell me about your drawing," you are modeling effective communication strategies, building the children's vocabularies, and demonstrating how to use language.

Research tells us that talking is one of the most important information processes in which a child can participate. Talking should occur in language-rich, information-rich conversations covering all subjects.[2] Extended conversations give children opportunities to listen to and practice narrative and explanatory talk.[3] These conversations can also contribute to a child's oral language and vocabulary. Conversations and talking between a parent and child can also provide information that contributes to the child's understanding of the language, beliefs, and behaviors of their cultures.[4]

What are the ways in which we talk with each other and with young children? We talk about simple, straightforward things—instructions on how to complete tasks, directions on how to get somewhere, a quick summary of a book for a patron. We also talk with parents about more complex, sophisticated things: why *Again!* by Emily Gravett[5] fits with other books a child has read and how the main character is going through situations familiar to a 4-year-old. We ask "what if," and we answer "why." And we encourage the children and adults who attend our storytimes to do the same.

WHY IS TALKING IMPORTANT?

According to the ECRR2 Toolkit, talking with children improves oral language, an important aspect of early literacy.[6] Furthermore, when children learn to express their thoughts and needs, this helps stimulate the brain, which is tied to all learning. Talking with children develops all aspects of early literacy, including print awareness, letter knowledge, phonological awareness, vocabulary, background knowledge, narrative skills, and print motivation. It is through talking that we purposefully call the child's attention to these aspects of language.

What we know is that *what* is discussed in conversations with children and how we talk with them are just as important—if not sometimes more important—than *how often* conversations happen.[7] Repeating the word *cat* sixty times doesn't result in a greater vocabulary; describing the cat as a soft, furry, small, long gray mammal with ears, paws, fur, a nose, and a mouth, gives children eleven additional words in one sentence. And this language is given in context, not as a list of vocabulary words to learn.

When we create teachable moments, we model those moments for the parents and caregivers. Furthermore, we demonstrate to children just how important conversations can be, as well as how to communicate needs, likes, and opinions using language. By doing this, we prepare children to develop their own talking skills, their own conversation styles, which is connected to the social aspect of learning and development. And this includes "parentese"—the singsong, exaggerated way we have of talking with our youngest attendees. Parentese signals to the baby that talking is a way of communicating, that something interesting is happening, that the sounds a baby makes are being heard and repeated. It is the source of a baby's first conversations, and it can help with language development. Even at 9 months, there is a beginning of a gap in words recognized based on the amount and kind of talk. This can be addressed through the use of parentese.[8]

It is important to note that while our own talking can help children develop language as they listen and note what we are drawing their attention to, the most powerful part of talking is encouraging children to express their own thoughts. This starts with infants, giving them time to babble back when we talk with them. For older children, we support their oral language development by allowing them time to share what they know and what they feel, perhaps when prompted by our open-ended questions, or time to ask questions about what is happening in a book or as part of a situation they observe.

Interactivity is infused into every domain, making it perhaps the most important vehicle for impacting the early literacy behaviors of children who attend storytime. Look for ways to interact with the children in your storytimes; give them a chance to respond to questions, finish rhymes, participate in conversations. They will learn so much more and feel a part of the storytime practice.

> I encourage kids to interact with me while I'm reading a book because I think that learning not only how to use critical thinking skills but how to express your thoughts and put them into words and interact actively with a story is really, really important.
>
> —Sara Lachman

VPT AND TALKING IN STORYTIMES: HOW DO I DO IT?

Children love to tell stories. They talk and share with little prompting. Our job is to help guide what they say back to the book or the rhyme while still validating their sharing and their lived experiences. This way we can build their vocabulary and enable their participation in a conversation, according to their stage of language development.

Even when we do not have time to have every child talk, we can encourage this practice by articulating quick examples, having "read-together time," or demonstrating how parents can ask open-ended questions when reading with their children one-on-one.

As you look at the VPT, you'll see certain verbs repeated throughout—*prompts, encourages, greets, responds, asks, invites.* These all indicate a use of talking to elicit a response, to highlight a concept, to share an experience, and to have a conversation.

We're going to examine one or two behaviors in each domain of the VPT to illustrate this approach. We encourage you to explore each domain on your own. Find a few behaviors that resonate with your participants and that match their developmental level and give them a try. You can always change things up, choose another behavior, and make your own choices as to how to implement this strategy.

Communication

Conversation is perhaps one of the most effective vehicles for transforming talking into communication. You want something, you ask someone for it, and that person gives it to you, perhaps talking a bit about it along the way. We use the phrase "how to talk and share" to speak colloquially about the Communication domain and what it means for your practice.

Some ways you communicate in your storytimes:

- Giving instructions for an activity. For instance, if you're giving instructions to jump like a frog in a movement rhyme, add open-ended questions such as, "Why is your frog jumping? What does he want? Where is he going?"
- Talking about the storytime theme and how it relates to children's lives. For instance, "Today we are talking about fall. What did you notice about the weather outside? Yes! It's chilly, isn't it? And windy and rainy. What about the leaves? They're changing colors. What do you think makes the leaves change color?" This kind of conversation shares essential information about a topic, boosts a child's vocabulary, and models talking as a way to convey an idea—also known as communication.

Look at the VPT under the domain of Communication:

- **With children ages birth to 18 months,** you can greet them using nonverbal gestures (which are also a form of communication) to support your verbal cues, and the children will use those gestures back to you, thus engaging in another kind of conversation.

- **With children ages 18 to 36 months,** you can provide opportunities for turn-taking conversations about the book you're reading or your storytime theme for the day; you will begin to see participation from the children in that conversation. Children just learning to have a conversation need more time than adults to respond. Even if it feels like the pause is too long, be sure to give them plenty of time to respond. And you can use your discretion, as you know your community best.
- **With children ages 36 to 60 months,** you can expand their understanding of communication by talking about the facial expressions of characters in a book and encouraging the children to make those expressions themselves, helping them realize that this is another way of communicating with others.

Language Use

You use language every day for many reasons and in many ways. You request, compliment, gather information, discuss, and instruct. We refer to the Language Use domain as "how to use words."

How do you use language in your storytimes? When you identify and label objects in illustrations, recite a rhyme and play with words, facilitate an action song through verbal instructions, and ask questions to check for understanding, you are modeling how to use language in various ways.

Look at the VPT under the domain of Language Use:

- **With children ages birth to 18 months of age,** you can recite an oral story or a nursery rhyme, demonstrating how language can be used in a narrative and playful way.
- **With children ages 18 to 36 months,** you can provide opportunities for fingerplays with songs and games, also using language in a playful way.
- **With children ages 36 to 30 months,** you can ask them to share a quick story about a recent event, perhaps something related to the theme of the day, and show them how to use language to recount an experience. If the group is large and you cannot listen to each child, you can provide a few minutes for them to "share in pairs" with another child or an adult.

Phonological Awareness

Talking is about stringing sounds together to make words and inserting pauses to create phrases and sentences. Encouraging children to become aware of these sounds and how different words can have similar sounds is part of promoting phonological awareness. We use the phrase "playing with sounds" to talk about the Phonological Awareness domain. Something as simple as clapping the syllables in words helps children hear the smaller sounds in words.

How do you play with sounds in your storytimes? Perhaps you encourage children to use sound effects when they do pretend play or as you're reading a book. If you feature a movement activity where the children are bees, they can buzz, buzz,

buzz all around just like bees. Pointing out the sound of the letter *b* in both *bees* and *buzz* and then emphasizing the sound that bees make—"buzz buzz"—encourages children to think about sounds in the words they use.

Look at the VPT under the domain of Phonological Awareness:

- **With children ages birth to 18 months,** you can use rhyme throughout your storytime to help them understand the sound and rhythm in language. This can also be done in a song, as there is natural overlap between the practices of talking and singing in storytimes.
- **With children ages 18 to 36 months,** you can invite them to clap out the syllables in words like *alphabet* or *caterpillar,* or you can have them clap very quickly or very slowly to learn about tempo through imitation.
- **With children ages 36 to 60 months,** you can encourage children to find multiple objects in an illustration that start with the same sound—*bee*, *bear*, *boat*, *bug*, *bat*. It is important to verbally label the pictures first so they hear the beginning sounds. You can then work with the children to help them find objects in a picture with the same beginning sound, with assistance.

Vocabulary

Vocabulary is perhaps one of the most natural domains that relates to the practice of talking. Consider the words you use when you describe the characters in the books you read. Could you point out the soft brown fur of the bear in *A Visitor for Bear*, by Bonny Becker?[9] The pinch-your-nose smelliness of the garbage truck in *I Stink!*, by Kate and Jim McMullan?[10] How freezing and wet and sticky the snow must be in *The Snowy Day*, by Ezra Jack Keats?[11] The more that you can assign descriptive words to the images the children see in the books you read, the more you will expose them to words they can then adopt and use themselves. Remember to use not only nouns and adjectives but also interesting verbs to describe movements as well as less common words for feelings depicted on the faces of characters, even if those words are not used in the text. Children will understand that the world around them is made up of things that have names, and that those names are words they can say and eventually read.

Vocabulary enters into all aspects of your storytime practice; fingerplays, action rhymes, and songs expose children to many different words. If you let the children finish each rhyme for you, you give even large groups a chance to participate, interact, and try out these words for themselves. Crafts and activities provide opportunities to build vocabulary as you give instructions and going around and talking with the children about the objects they're creating. You're providing new words and eliciting words from them in the stories they tell. Keep in mind that when children speak, they are using words they already know. You are building their vocabulary by adding to what they say, by using a less familiar synonym, and by expanding on their ideas. For babies, all words are new and they need a lot of repetition to learn. As children get older, they need more than just to hear words—they need to hear a new or less familiar word used in context, as they are experiencing a particular situation, so that they learn how a word is used. Preschoolers benefit from a little explanation between the meanings of similar words. Again, this is a way they learn more about their world.

Look at the VPT under the Vocabulary domain:

- **With children ages birth to 18 months,** you can identify familiar objects in a book or in the room and invite the children to point to familiar objects. Eventually you'll start to hear them use these familiar words themselves.
- **With children ages 18 to 36 months,** you can invite them to use adjectives to describe objects or things described in stories, and you can eventually expect to see the children using adjectives in their phrases. As you do an activity in storytime, ask them to give you the words from time to time; if they have trouble, give them the word and encourage them to repeat what you say.
- **With children ages 36 to 60 months,** you can model using multiple words to explain ideas. For instance, you could say, "Another way to say 'soft brown bear' is 'plush brown bear' or 'furry brown bear.' Another way to say 'hungry' is 'ravenous' or 'starving.'" Or you might ask, "What is the difference between being hungry and being ravenous?"

Remind parents and caregivers that children need repetition to learn. This doesn't mean just saying a word over and over, but rather talking about an object as they point to it or talk about it.

Additionally, a recent study noted that babies use their names as an anchor to help them understand the next word.[12] So, if we say, "Nathan, here is your blanket," Nathan pays the most attention to the first word after his name—in this case, *here*. We would rather he pay attention to the more important word, *blanket*. So it makes more sense to say, "Nathan, blanket—here is your warm, fuzzy blanket." It is also natural that adults mostly use the names of objects for babies. However, it is important to use all kinds of words with babies, not just items they can see. So, if a baby is looking at a picture of a dog, for example, the baby needs to hear more than just "dog" or "woof, woof." The adult can talk about a dog she had as a child or tell a story about the dog in the picture, giving the baby exposure to many words, whether he understands them or not. In many cases you'll see that in these domains, providing the opportunity to use the concept—in this case, vocabulary—is vitally important and linked to improvement in that area.

Comprehension

How do you make sure that others understand you and your requests are met? You use the right words in the right order to communicate your thoughts. Comprehension, vocabulary, and communication are all related. We refer to the Comprehension domain as "understanding words, stories, directions, ideas, etc."

How do you facilitate comprehension in your storytime? "Today we're going to read a book about an apple. Do you see an apple on this page? Who likes to eat apples? I'm holding a juicy, red apple in my hand and I'm going to bite into this apple. Let's pretend you're holding a juicy red apple, too. Let me see you bite into your apples. Mmm, how does it taste? Let me see you eat a second apple. How many apples do you think you can eat today? What can we make out of apples?" Through this conversation, you're providing vocabulary; you're communicating different concepts around the object of an apple; and you're facilitating the children's comprehension of apple as something you can eat, something you can point out in a picture, and something you can talk about and relate to the children's experiences.

Look at the VPT under the domain of Comprehension:

- **With children ages birth to 18 months,** you can label objects and use descriptions as well. You can use words to give one-step directions and give them time to respond, either verbally or nonverbally. The children will respond appropriately to familiar words and follow single-step directions.
- **With children ages 18 to 36 months,** you can use a conversation to facilitate comprehension. The conversation can be as you introduce a book, talking about an idea or concept, or helping children relate to something that occurs in the book. It can be around the storytime theme or as you do a craft or activity.
- **With children ages 36 to 60 months,** you can push their boundaries by introducing made-up words and talk about the differences between "real" and "made-up" words in terms of understanding what they mean. This will help children distinguish between "real" and "made-up" words.

Print Concepts

In storytimes, you use print in the form of the books you read. When you lay out an array of board and cloth books for babies to explore and hold and chew on, you provide the children with an opportunity to explore. Though perhaps not what we would traditionally consider to be reading, this exploration enables young children to interact with books, to hold them and play with them as objects, and to understand how they work—all of which has an impact on later interactions with print. We refer to the Print Concepts domain as connecting with books and stories.

How do you facilitate a connection with print in your storytimes? Discussing the cover image of a book, using that image to help the children predict what the story might be about, running your finger under the text in the title or a repeated phrase in the book, pointing out the author and illustrator of the book—all of these are ways you are helping children develop proficiency with print.

Look at the VPT under the domain of Print Concepts:

- **With children ages birth to 18 months,** you can point to the pictures and label them as you read. You may bring in an actual item and then show the picture to help them understand that the picture is representing the actual object. As you say a repeated phrase in the book, you can point to each word in the text. You can also talk about the objects and characters in an illustration, further engaging the children with the print object.
- **With children ages 18 to 36 months,** you can ask questions about the story that encourage the children to imagine what might happen next, and then pause to let them respond. Pausing is key here—it provides an interactive atmosphere and lets the children know it's their turn to participate. As you

say a repeated phrase, you can point to each word in the text. You can also talk about the objects and characters in an illustration, further engaging the children with the print object.

- **With children ages 36 to 60 months,** you can talk about signs in the books you read and ask the children if they recognize the signs from their everyday experiences, encouraging them to engage with print in the outside world. Print is all around us, and you can help them see that and begin to decode their world. If a word is written in a font that indicates how to say the word or phrase in a certain way, point that out. For example, a word written in larger or bolded type would be said louder than the surrounding words.

Alphabetic Knowledge

Together with Phonological Awareness, the Alphabetic Knowledge domain has been shown in research studies to be a predictor of the decoding aspect of later reading readiness. These two areas were also emphasized in the VIEWS2 study as important areas to focus on in storytime. We refer to the Alphabetic Knowledge domain as exploring with letters. However, there are two concepts that are in fact precursors to alphabetic knowledge: shapes and alike and different. Children identify letters by their shapes, so a *c* is a circle with a hole in it, or a *d* is a circle with a line coming out of it. Because many letters look alike, such as a lowercase *n* and a lowercase *h*, children must also learn to discern visual differences and similarities between objects. Matching games support this concept.

How do you explore with letters in your storytime? Whenever you point out the shape of an object, when you encourage the children to make a letter shape with their bodies, when you do a fingerplay with shapes, when you put a felt letter on the board and encourage the children to identify that letter in the activities you provide, you're emphasizing alphabetic knowledge.

Look at the VPT under the domain of Alphabetic Knowledge:

- **With children ages birth to 18 months,** you can read books that have repetitive sounds in them, such as *In the Small, Small Pond,* by Denise Fleming.[13] Children will imitate the sounds when looking at the words in the book.
- **With children ages 18 to 36 months,** you can ask them to find a letter or a word on a page of the book you're reading, helping them to distinguish art and text and understand that print represents words. You can even encourage them to pretend to read the text.
- **With children ages 36 to 60 months,** you can point to each word separately as you read and prompt children to identify the same word across pages of a book.

You can also incorporate alphabetic knowledge into the rhymes and songs you do by singing the alphabet song or spelling out a word on the felt board and then doing a rhyme or a song about that word, such as *boat* and "Row, Row, Row Your Boat." This is an example of how Phonological Awareness and Alphabetic Knowledge domains often overlap in the practice of talking in storytimes.

Writing Concepts

Historically, writing in the traditional sense has not been included regularly in storytime activities. However, you may be surprised to see that in fact you are incorporating writing concepts into the activities you already do. When you point out text as separate from pictures in a book with little ones, you're helping them distinguish the information on a page. When you move your finger along with the text as you read, you're demonstrating to children that the text moves from left to right and that those symbols represent information that is written and can be read.

Look at the VPT under the domain of Writing Concepts:

- **With children ages birth to 18 months,** encourage them to point to the text on a page of a book, to help them think about the difference between art and text.
- **With children ages 18 to 36 months**, ask them about the scribbling they do on their name tags or during crafts and point to text while it is being read out loud—you're demonstrating to them that we hear and see words. You are also validating the writing they've done as representational of an idea.
- **With children ages 36 to 60 months,** encourage them to identify a letter and then to look for that letter in the print around them, perhaps on signs in the storytime room or in other books they read. The children will learn to identify letters that match the spoken letter name. You may see some overlap here with the behaviors under Alphabetic Knowledge. For very young children, letters and early writing are linked.

With a big group, you could encourage this skill by pointing to different spaces on a page and having the children shout out when you are pointing to text. Writing comes with practice; you can help the children discover the practice of writing through a specific storytime activity. You can talk the children through painting letters in the air—they can choose colors for their "paint" and then paint big letters in the air or tiny letters on their bodies.

A WORD FROM THE EXPERT　　　　　　　　SARA LACHMAN

■ Talking and Interactivity

I feel like sometimes reading is treated like this kind of formal sit-down thing. This is listening time and not fun [or] playtime. [But] reading can be play, too. And I think talking about what you're reading as you're doing it is what makes it fun. It's a social skill, too, like learning how to take turns in a conversation.

■ Tips for Talking

I make sure that I pick books that have a lot to talk about in them—books that have actual stories or are complex in some way and that have [some] ambiguity, or where the pictures are just as important as the words. Then we can actually talk about how the words and the pictures work together to create the story.

I also play a lot of interactive talking games. I always start my storytimes by talking about the theme. I know a lot of librarians don't do themes, and I don't think themes are necessary, but I really like them for creating conversations because before we read the books, we talk about the themes. So if my theme is names—I did a name storytime, for example—we talk about what our names are, and if anyone has a nickname, then I explain the concept of nicknames. And we talk about that before we start. So they're already in the mindset of understanding what we are doing for the day.

Every time we come across a hard word in a book, we stop and we try saying it together. That way we experience the fun of saying long, complicated words together. I'm constantly finding ways for them to be talking to me about a book instead of me just standing in front of them and reading.

I focus a lot on what is actually happening in the story, and I like making connections to their real lives. I pull in what's happening to the characters and whether stuff like that happens to them. I also point out repeating words a lot—if the title is a repeating refrain, I'll teach them what the word looks like, and then every time we see the word in the book, we all say it together.

■ Talking with Different Age Groups

With toddlers, I would ask concrete questions about their own experiences and their preferences—questions like, "What do you see on this page?" "What is happening on this page?" "What color is this?" Really concrete things that show that I'm welcoming them to talk to me, but [using] easier concepts that they can actually understand.

And then, for even younger kids who aren't even talking yet, I just leave a space in the interaction to show that it's a two-sided conversation. For instance, I read a page and now it's your turn to react, whatever reacting means for you, like making silly noises or clapping, just to make it clear that reading is a conversation. It's not a one-sided thing.

■ How to Share with Parents/Caregivers about Talking

I think it's really important for parents to see that if their kid is interacting with me, I'm not annoyed at them for interrupting. I think a lot of parents have this idea that storytime is where you go to sit and listen and be quiet. If a kid talks to me, I will respond. It makes me really excited and happy when they do that because it means that they're actively engaged in what I'm doing.

So I model how to read a book interactively and then gently reassure the parents that it's okay for storytime to be interactive. Because I think that's the biggest thing I come across—parents are terrified of their kids interrupting and causing a fuss. So I just reassure [parents] that that's what I want. I design my storytime so that [the children] will do that and if it happens, it's my fault, not their kids and that it's a good thing. It means that they're engaged.

TALKING AND SCAFFOLDING

With talking, we are intentionally trying to give children opportunities to talk. Therefore it is important to understand at each stage what their "talking" might be like so that you can best support it. Babies may "talk" by babbling, cooing, and crying. Toddlers will say some words and sentences, but we may not completely understand them all. Preschoolers can usually engage in a short conversation and can use longer sentences with more detail.

What is most important with talking is that we expose children to rich language and give them many opportunities to talk in whatever form they can use at that stage. You can support their talking by:

- babbling back at babies;
- introducing sign language and gestures for children who do not yet use words or whose words you cannot yet understand;
- labeling objects for young children who have smaller vocabularies;
- providing lots of opportunities for preschoolers to talk and share about books and their daily lives; and
- talking about not only the present but past and future happenings, too.

- **With children ages birth to 18 months.** When reading a book, you can pause after talking about a page to give the babies time to babble back. Once they do babble at you, make sure to respond to them. When reading, you can also walk around with the book and get close to each baby individually, taking a second to show the baby the page and talk to him or her directly.

  When labeling items, babies pay most attention to the first word after their name, so make a point to say the most important word after calling their name. Remember this example from earlier in this chapter: "Nathan, blanket—this is your warm, fuzzy blanket." Teaching this technique to caregivers will offer them ways to specifically support talking.
- **With children ages 18 to 36 months.** When reading a book, toddlers can say a repeated phrase so have them chime in with a repeated word or phrase in the story. Also, prompt them to labels lots of pictures in the books, as it will help build their vocabulary.

  At this stage repetition is especially important, so use repetition for anything you incorporate—for example, fingerplays or songs—that gets them talking. Have them repeat after you and then repeat the fingerplay or song a couple of times during the storytime and across multiple storytimes.
- **With children ages 36 to 60 months.** When reading a book, you can also have preschoolers chime in with a repeated phrase, but try using a longer phrase or one that contains more complex words than what you use with toddlers. You can also ask preschoolers to recount part of the story or predict what will happen next, as this gives them a chance to work on their talking skills.

You can also engage preschoolers in a conversation during storytime. Encourage them to share information they know about a topic or the storytime theme. You might offer an opportunity for children to tell their adult a story of their own using the characters in a book you read during storytime.

Talking to and with children is critical to all later language development, early literacy, and reading literacy. By re-examining and expanding the ways we talk informally with each child even before storytime begins, by intentionally seeking ways to make storytimes more interactive, and by pointing out rich ways to talk with children to the parents and caregivers, we can make powerful differences from the opportunities we have.

NOTES

1. After graduating from the University of Washington's iSchool, Sara Lachman has been working as a youth services librarian since 2010. She enjoys working with preschoolers all the way up through teenagers, playing overly complicated board games, watching horror movies, and eating cheese.
2. Catherine E. Snow, Patton O. Tabors, and David K. Dickinson, "Language Development in the Preschool Years." In *Beginning Literacy with Language*, ed. David K. Dickinson and Patton O. Tabors (Baltimore: Paul H. Brookes, 2001), 1–25.
3. Diane E. Beals, "Eating and Reading: Links between Family Conversations with Preschoolers and Later Language and Literacy," in *Beginning Literacy with Language*, ed. David K. Dickinson and Patton O. Tabors (Baltimore: Paul H. Brookes, 2001), 75–92.
4. Ibid.
5. Emily Gravett, *Again!* (New York: Simon & Schuster Books for Young Readers, 2013).
6. Association for Library Services to Children (ALSC) and Public Library Association (PLA), *Every Child Ready to Read, 2nd Edition Kit*, 2011, section 1, 5.
7. Anne Fernald, "How Talking to Children Nurtures Language Development across SES and Culture," paper presented at the 2014 AAAS Annual Meeting, Chicago, February 14, https://aaas.confex.com/aaas/2014/webprogram/Paper11747.html.
8. Nairán Ramírez-Esparza, Adrián García-Sierra, and Patricia K. Kuhl, "Look Who's Talking: Speech Style and Social Context in Language Input to Infants Are Linked to Concurrent and Future Speech Development," *Developmental Science* 17, no. 6 (2014): 880–91, doi:10.1111/desc.12172.
9. Bonny Becker, *A Visitor for Bear*, illus. Kady MacDonald Denton (Cambridge, MA: Candlewick Press, 2008).
10. Kate McMullan, *I Stink!*, illus. Jim McMullan (New York: Joanna Cotler Books, 2002).
11. Ezra Jack Keats, *The Snowy Day* illus. by the author (New York: Viking Press, 1962).
12. Heather Bortfeld, James L. Morgan, Roberta Michnick Golinkoff, and Karen Rathbun, "Mommy and Me: Familiar Names Help Launch Babies into Speech-Stream Segmentation," *Psychological Science* 16, no. 4 (2005): 298–304.
13. Denise Fleming, *In the Small, Small Pond*, illus. by the author (New York: Henry Holt, 1993).

WORKSHEET

Reflection Questions on Talking

1. What is the target age group of my storytimes?

   _____

2. What age groups actually attend my storytimes?

   _____

3. How do I model talking to fit the age group(s) of the children who attend my story-times, using behaviors from the VPT?

   _____

   _____

4. How have I been successful in doing so?

   _____

   _____

5. How do I model interactivity through talking in my storytime?

   _____

   _____

6. How have I been successful in doing so?

   _____

   _____

7. How do I provide children with opportunities to talk and participate in conversations in my storytime?

   _____

   _____

8. How do I scaffold talking activities for different ages and abilities in my storytime?

   _____

   _____

9. How do I talk with parents/caregivers about talking with their child(ren)?

   _____

   _____

10. What would I change for a future storytime to incorporate behaviors around talking interactively in my storytime?

    _____

    _____

11. How do I incorporate fun into my talking activities?

    _____

    _____

READING

The act of reading is important for so many reasons—there's no way that I could list them all! One of my favorite things about reading in storytime is that I get to show families how much fun reading together can be. I choose books that I love so much that I just can't wait to share them. I know that reading is great for kids' brains and it gives them new words, and I want my excitement about books and sharing stories to be infectious. I want both the kids and the adults to leave my programs thinking that reading books together is fantastic!

—Mari Nowitz, Youth Services Librarian, Tumwater Timberland Library[1]

EADING IS AN ICONIC PART OF STORYTIMES. EVEN THE word *storytime* denotes the telling of stories, many of which are print-based. Many people immediately think of the image of a storytime provider sitting in a chair, reading to children who are nestled near her in a semicircle on a brightly colored rug. In addition, when people think of early literacy, they immediately think of books and reading with children. In the course of observing storytimes for Project VIEWS2, we found storytime providers still love to read classic favorites and brand-new gems. However, there is one big difference: whereas before, reading a story meant performing or presenting it for the children, nowadays reading is transforming into a participatory, interactive experience that offers incredible opportunities for incorporating a variety of early literacy behaviors.

Essentially you are infusing interactivity into the reading process. It is "the language and the social interaction that surrounds the book during the reading . . . [that] causes storybook reading to be so powerful an activity for young children."[2] By reading interactively with children, you are encouraging many different types of early literacy skills. Children learn best when they are actively engaged in helping to tell the story.

> It's really interesting to watch kids as they go through a year or two of storytimes where they are asked questions during the stories. Many, especially young kids, will start out being unable (or unwilling) to answer. Eventually, I can see them thinking about my questions and evaluating what is happening during the story. It's really amazing to watch that learning happen.
>
> —Mari Nowitz

Interactive Reading

Reading interactively in storytime can happen in many different ways. With pre-school children, one of the easiest methods is to ask questions about the book. There are many types of questions you can ask. Be sure to pause to give the children time to respond. Remember, you do not have to interrupt the story if you do not want to. You can come back to a page to ask questions.

- While showing the front cover of a book to the children, ask what they think the story will be about.
- Point out a picture and ask the children to describe what they think is happening in the picture.
- When reading a part of a book, ask the children if they have ever done something similar.
- When you are further along in the book, ask the children a question about a previous event in the book.

With younger children, you can ask them to repeat words or sounds from the book or to identify pictures in the book. You can also have them act out things from the book—for example, swaying like a tree in the wind. Taking the time to introduce a repeated phrase or action before starting to read the book and having them practice it makes it more likely that they will participate during the reading.

We know from research that including informational books along with picture books is an excellent way to encourage interactivity, especially between parents and children. Informational books invite pauses, questions, and interaction in a way that fictional picture books do not as much; with picture books, parents can sometimes feel pressured to forge ahead and get to the end of a story, perhaps to show children how a story works, perhaps to combat natural wiggliness. An informational book, on the other hand, enables a back-and-forth reading style filled with rich language and taking turns—perfect for interactive reading!

Dialogic Reading

Dialogic reading is an interactive reading technique developed in the education field that builds on the practice of asking children questions about the book. This technique involves encouraging children to talk about the story and the pictures by asking them questions and providing feedback that extends the children's statements.[3] There are many types of questions that you can ask to engage the children in the story. A good place to start is using *wh-* questions: who, what, when, where, and why (see the sidebar for additional types of prompts to use). Through dialogic reading, you are essentially asking the children to help you tell the story. This technique is an example of how the practices of reading and talking overlap.

While dialogic reading is most commonly associated with one-on-one reading with a child, research has demonstrated that dialogic reading techniques can be used effectively with groups of children to encourage interactions and to keep them engaged.[5] By using these techniques in storytime, you have the benefit of pointing out and explaining to caregivers what the techniques are and why you are using them, so that they can do them at home with their children.

DIALOGIC READING PROMPTS

There are five types of prompts that work well for reading interactively and incorporating dialogic reading techniques in your storytimes. The acronym CROWD offers a great way to remember the five types of prompts.[4]

- **C**ompletion prompts: provide a sentence and let the children fill in the last word (this technique works really well for rhymes).
- **R**ecall prompts: ask the children questions about what has happened previously in the story.
- **O**pen-ended prompts: ask the children to describe what is happening in a story.
- **W**h- prompts: asking the children questions that start with *who, what, when, where,* and *why*.
- **D**istancing prompts: ask the children to relate a piece of the story to things that they have experienced.

The acronym PEER offers a great way to remember the different steps in dialogic reading.[6]

- **P**rompt the children to tell you something about the book by asking a question.
- **E**valuate the children's responses by saying something like, "That's right!"
- **E**xpand the children's responses by repeating what they said and adding information to it.
- **R**epeat the beginning question for the children and give them a chance to answer with the expanded detail.

A basic example of how to do this for younger children using the book *I Stink!* by Kate and Jim McMullan:[7]

1. Point to the truck and ask the children, "What is this?"
2. Allow the children time to respond with, "A truck."
3. Respond to the children with something like, "That's right, a stinky garbage truck."
4. Ask the children, "What is it again?" to allow them to repeat the expanded detail.

The key to dialogic reading techniques is making sure to pause to give the children time to respond and following their lead, as well as expanding on the children's comments and asking additional questions to extend the conversation with the children. You want the process to be as interactive as possible because the children will learn more by engaging with you and the book.

Print Referencing

Print referencing is another reading technique developed in the education field that can be used in storytimes. Print referencing is the practice of calling attention to and talking about print using verbal and nonverbal methods. Print referencing can be done with books, magazines, posters, flannelboards, digital devices—essentially anything that has letters and words. Print referencing works well for encouraging children's print concept and alphabet knowledge.[8]

You are using *nonverbal* methods of print referencing when you:

- track the print in a book as you read it;
- point to specific words as you read them—like a repetitive phrase you are having the children repeat; or
- point to letters in a book or on a flannelboard as you discuss them.

You are using *verbal* methods of print referencing when you:

- ask children to find a letter in print;
- ask children to identify a letter;
- point to a letter and talk about its shape; or
- call attention to words and how they may look different from each other.

> In my storytimes, I try and make sure that there are times where even pre-readers have a positive experience with a physical book that they're touching, holding, and being able to interact with.
>
> —Mari Nowitz

DIALOGIC READING TECHNIQUES IN LARGE GROUPS

While dialogic reading is best known as a one-on-one approach, the principles can be incorporated into larger storytimes. For instance, you can ask open-ended questions about the book you're reading. This also models for parents how to use dialogic reading techniques at home with their own child or children.

Whatever techniques you decide to use in your reading, the main thing to remember is to involve the children—through questions, acting out pieces from the book, repeating phrases, and identifying pictures and print. Don't forget to follow the children's lead, pausing to give them time to respond to you and further responding to them by evaluating and expanding on what they've said. Remember that by incorporating interactivity in your reading, you are increasing the opportunities for the children to learn important early literacy skills.

WHY IS READING IMPORTANT?

According to the ECRR2 Toolkit, shared reading has an incredible impact on helping children become skilled readers.[9] Similar to talking, reading also includes all of the early literacy skills. And *how* we read with children is just as important—if not sometimes more important—than *how often* we read with children.

Reading, overall, is crucial because it helps develop children's listening skills and exposes them to vocabulary not typically used in conversations, print concepts, and background knowledge. Infusing interactivity into your storytime reading practices—for example, asking older children to predict what is going to happen in a story or having younger children repeat phrases—is key to encouraging many other early literacy skills, such as oral language, narrative, and vocabulary skills. These interactive practices help children internalize the story and support their comprehension skills.

Some of the most significant impacts of dialogic reading are on the child's oral language and vocabulary skills. Well-developed oral language skills and a rich oral vocabulary will contribute to children's later reading skills because if they are familiar with and know how to use the words they are trying to read, it is easier for them to recognize the words as they sound out the letters. Dialogic reading contributes to oral language and oral vocabulary by giving the child an opportunity to practice with language skills and unfamiliar words when responding to the prompts. The follow-up evaluation helps to solidify the current concepts and vocabulary, while the follow-up expansion helps introduce new concepts and vocabulary.

Using print referencing in storytime can support the development of children's print concept and alphabet knowledge skills. We highlight this because during Project VIEWS2, alphabetic knowledge skills were observed during only a small percentage of storytimes. Given that alphabetic knowledge is a strong predictor of later reading success, it is an important skill to include in storytimes. Providing fun and enjoyable ways to expose children to information about letters through print referencing can provide the foundation for this skill.

Using different techniques for reading in storytime is also important on another level because you are demonstrating to caregivers *how* to read with young children. As you employ the different techniques, you can also use asides to explain why you are using that technique. By reading interactively, you are showing the caregivers that it is beneficial for the child when they to stop and talk about pieces of the story and ask their child questions; that it is okay to not read the story word for word; and that it is most important to follow the child's lead and let them be involved in telling the story.

VPT AND READING IN STORYTIMES: HOW DO I DO IT?

On a basic level, reading is very simple to do. You open a book, you begin on page 1, and you carry your young, wriggly audience off to a fantastical world, deep into a dark forest or off in a boat on the high seas. The cadence and inflection of your voice and the rich vocabulary you use will stimulate a child's imagination and bring the story to life for them. As we've mentioned, inserting pauses and allowing children time to reflect and interact with a story—even just a little bit at a time—will take your reading to the next level. While this practice may seem difficult with a big group, you can ask the whole group a question and let them shout back. Storytimes need be neither quiet nor orderly when interactivity and dialogic reading techniques are being done well!

Communication

As we saw in the talking chapter, communication means putting thoughts into words and putting those words together in a clear way to facilitate understanding. The same is true for reading. When you encounter text of any kind, print or digital, you understand it best when it communicates concisely and effectively.

When you choose a book to read in storytime, you read through it first and make sure it's age appropriate and easy to understand for your young audience. You can also look for opportunities to enable your audience to talk and share along with the story. In this way, you're demonstrating that reading is a way of communicating ideas, stories, and messages.

Look at the VPT under the domain of Communication:

- **With children ages birth to 18 months,** you can insert pauses as you read to give the little ones a chance to respond. They might only babble or coo, but they are letting you know they have something to add; you want to give them the space for that.
- **With children ages 18 to 36 months,** you can pause as well, giving these older ones the chance to respond to a question like, "What did you like about the book?"
- **With children ages 36 to 60 months,** you can encourage them to express their opinions, their likes and dislikes, about the books, helping them to communicate and develop their own ideas.

Language Use

When you use language that enhances and expands the stories you read in a storytime, you're modeling for parents/caregivers and children alike that language can be used in various ways.

Perhaps you ask children to describe the characters they see on the cover of *A Visitor for Bear*, by Bonny Becker;[10] you can also ask them to predict what will happen next. Encourage children to repeat the recurring phrase "Bear says thanks" as you read Karma Wilson's book.[11] These are additional ways in which you are putting language to use for multiple purposes.

Thinking about the way I plan my storytimes and the way I relate to my storytime groups, the thing I feel is maybe the most important is getting across how much *fun* books are. Of course reading is important because it helps make lots of connections in kids' brains and helps develop the skills they will need in their later learning. But for me, the root of helping create lifelong readers and learners is figuring out how to help children discover that books are wonderful.

—Mari Nowitz

Look at the VPT under the domain of Language Use:

- **With children ages birth to 18 months,** you can tell a story orally—perhaps using puppets or a flannelboard—to encourage them to listen to oral stories and use language to express simple ideas.
- **With children ages 18 months to 36 months,** you can prompt them to think about the sequence of the events in the story, to help them develop an understanding of language through listening.
- **With children ages 36 to 60 months,** ask them to talk about a specific detail or event in the books you read. This will encourage them to respond to questions with appropriate answers.

Phonological Awareness

Children are listening to the sounds of the words when you read. Rhyming books present excellent opportunities to focus on phonological awareness when you're reading in your storytime. Not only are you exposing children to new types of stories and reading opportunities, but you are also underscoring word play and the sounds of words in text.

When you choose books that feature onomatopoeia, children have the opportunity to imitate the sounds in the text and learn that sounds can be words. *In the Small, Small Pond,* by Denise Fleming,[12] is filled with wonderful rhyming words and onomatopoeic words that are fun to say and even more fun to repeat: "In the small, small pond, wiggle, jiggle, tadpoles wriggle." This phrase can bring in vocabulary, comprehension, and phonological awareness as you encourage children to say "wiggle, jiggle." And chances are, you'll make them giggle, too!

Look at the VPT under the domain of Phonological Awareness:

- **With children ages birth to 18 months,** you can read developmentally appropriate books and provide time for the children to insert familiar words. This is perhaps most easily done with rhyming books, as the children can then learn to match word sounds.
- **With children ages 18 to 36 months,** you can do this same activity, perhaps more frequently and with more complex rhymes.
- **With children ages 36 to 60 months,** you can make the sound recognition activity significantly more advanced by asking them to think about words that have similar sounds, such as *three* and *tree*—they sound similar but not exactly the same. Children will learn to differentiate between similar-sounding words.

Vocabulary

Reading involves words and sometimes pictures, but it is the words that you read out loud. Those words represent images, actions, places, people—and they have incredible power. Your young audience is listening to the words you read and undertaking the difficult task of making meaning from those words. So when you choose books that have unfamiliar language, you're opening up new vocabulary for them. If you stop to explain some of the words, you give them a context that resonates for young children to help them understand and make meaning for themselves.

Vocabulary isn't just about difficult or unfamiliar words; you can also introduce made-up words with preschoolers in your storytime activities. This will help the children learn how to be flexible with language and comprehension—showing how the Vocabulary domain can overlap with Comprehension and Language Use.

Look at the VPT under the Vocabulary domain:

You'll see behaviors that involve *labeling, prompting, asking questions, using adjectives, sharing stories*, and *modeling using words* to explain ideas. All of these represent opportunities to build a child's vocabulary.

- **With children ages birth to 18 months,** you can use gestures along with the words you're using so that the meaning comes across more clearly. The children will then learn to use and understand gestures and words to communicate.
- **With children ages 18 to 36 months,** you can use a simple three- to four-word sentence at least twice, followed by a pause so that the children can repeat it, and you can look for repetition of that phrase in your audience. This gives the children a chance to try out the vocabulary you've modeled and to hear others say the words, too.
- **With children ages 36 to 60 months,** you can encourage them to share how they feel about a particular event in a story, enabling them to draw on their own vocabulary. You might then expand on what they say. Additionally, you can include wordless picture books in your storytime and then use rich language as you tell the story. In this way you can build both vocabulary and comprehension.

Comprehension

Meaning making, something we just talked about under Vocabulary, also falls under the Comprehension domain. When we are faced with a passage of text, which words do we know and understand? Which words are unfamiliar, and how do we understand what we read amidst all those various words? Young children face this problem regularly as they listen to and begin to decode print.

When you read, for instance, *Where the Wild Things Are*, by Maurice Sendak,[13] and you come to the passage that reads, "They roared their terrible roars and gnashed their terrible teeth," you can ask children what they think "terrible" means, or "gnashed." What would it look like to gnash your teeth? Would it make a loud sound or a quiet sound? Why do you think they are roaring and gnashing their teeth? When you point to the illustrations and ask about the expressions on the wild things' faces, you are modeling how to use context clues to make meaning and develop a possible meaning for unfamiliar words. Plus, it's just plain fun to be a wild thing!

Look at the VPT under the domain of Comprehension:

- **With children ages birth to 18 months,** you can focus more on simple directions and gesturing toward an object; the children will pay attention to the object and point to it when it is named. In this way you're emphasizing both vocabulary and comprehension.

- **With children ages 18 to 36 months,** you can ask questions during reading to elicit short verbal answers and assess whether they understand the story. You can use humor to do this in a soft, gentle way.
- **With children ages 36 to 60 months,** provide opportunities for them to ask questions or reflect and share on an event in the story you're reading; the children will ask questions that demonstrate knowledge of events. You could ask a question like, "What do you think 'rumpus' means, and have you ever made a rumpus?" Be ready to explain further if perhaps some children need a little help. We want to help them feel good about every interaction with print and story. And remember to pause, pause, pause—give your audience a moment to respond.

Print Concepts

A natural domain for the practice of reading, Print Concepts is about helping children to develop a love of books and stories. Libraries do this through their extensive collections and children's programming. You do this in your storytimes when you read and tell stories. You can also provide an environment filled with different kinds of print for children to interact with and read.

Look at the VPT under the domain of Print Concepts:

- **With children ages birth to 18 months**, provide an array of books for the children to look at before or after storytime, perhaps even having books for all the infants and toddlers in your lapsit storytime. You're presenting children with the opportunity to explore books as part of a hands-on activity, an essential prereading skill.
- **With children ages 18 to 36 months** (especially if you have a smaller group), encourage them to think about the story you're reading in terms of other books they've read. They can also think about specific characters from those books, particularly with familiar stories. "Have you read other books about bears? What story has three bears in it? How many bears are in this story? What was your favorite thing about the bear in this story?"
- **With children ages 36 to 60 months**, think about including some informational books in your storytime, especially ones with environmental print such as street signs. This is an excellent way to bring the outside world into storytime and give the kids an awareness that can continue when they leave the library.

Alphabetic Knowledge

Reading is a natural venue for emphasizing the Alphabetic Knowledge domain, and yet, it's not necessary to have alphabet books to achieve this. In fact, you can bring STEM (science, technology, engineering, and math) concepts into this domain as well. Recognizing geometric shapes helps with recognizing letter shapes.

In your storytime, you can provide an environment in which children can explore with letters and begin to decode the world around them one letter at a time. Emphasizing the first letter of a child's first name is a way to introduce this exploration. You might also look for ways to overlap Phonological Awareness and Alphabetic Knowledge domains by highlighting, for instance, the letter *s*, the sound that letter makes, and how that sound is similar to the noise a snake makes, and the word *snake* starts with an *s*!

Look at the VPT under the domain of Alphabetic Knowledge:

- **With children ages birth to 18 months,** you can read a book slowly and deliberately, pronouncing each word, and give them a chance to imitate the words you're reading when looking at the words in the book.
- **With children ages 18 to 36 months,** ask them to find the print on a page of a book you're reading to help them understand that print represents words.
- **With children ages 36 to 60 months,** you can point out the shapes of specific letters on a flannelboard you're using: uppercase *B*'s and *D*'s have round shapes; *K*'s and *T*'s are made up only of lines; and so on.

Writing Concepts

Reading and writing might seem as though they don't fit together in a storytime, and they might feel too close to formal school. In fact, in your storytimes, you have the perfect opportunity to develop prewriting skills every time you read by distinguishing print and pictures and pointing to letters and words as you read. Take time to talk about the author and illustrator of the book. You can help kids understand and realize that someone wrote the words of the book, someone drew the pictures,

BOOK BABIES BOOK SETS

A couple of years ago, my colleague Elizabeth Moss had this great idea for presenting baby storytimes. She would reserve many copies of the book that she was going to share in storytime, making sure that each family (or each pair of families) in the circle had a book to look at. Then she would lead everyone in reading the story out loud together. Our youth services coordinator, Ellen Duffy, liked that idea so much that she put together a number of Book Babies book sets.

Our library system now has tubs of books that storytime providers can reserve [with] fifteen copies each of the same title. Many of them are board books, which means parents and caregivers can enjoy the reading experience without worrying about ripped pages. I love using these kits! When we read our story all together as a group, the babies can really interact with the books and see the pages up close. The older babies get to turn the pages, point at the pictures and words, or crawl across the room to look at somebody else's book. As we read together, I'll model dialogic reading and very briefly explain why it is so great for the babies. I love prompting the adults to ask questions like, "What's happening on this page?" and seeing how the caregivers respond to their children.

This type of book sharing incorporates a lot of the things that I recognize from [the VPT]. It feels so immediate and interactive because the book is right there in their hands. As the weeks progress and the adults get more comfortable with asking questions as we read, while leaving space for their children to respond, I can build in other literacy elements for them to watch me model and then try themselves.

—MARI NOWITZ

and these two aspects fit together to make the story you're reading and sharing in your storytime. Writing helps create the content you read.

Look at the VPT under the domain of Writing Concepts:

- **With children ages birth to 18 months,** you can point to a word or a line of text in the book you're reading or follow along with your finger as you read from right to left. You're modeling for the children that text moves in a particular direction in the book you're reading, and you're modeling for parents how they can emphasize this when they read at home.
- **With children ages 18 to 36 months,** try choosing a particular letter on a page that has big, bold text and trace the letter with your finger. In this way you're "writing" the letter on the page and reinforcing the act of writing as you're reading.
- **With children ages 36 to 60 months,** you might connect your reading activity with a craft and ask some dialogic questions that prompt them to think up their own story. Then they can tell their story to their caregiver during the craft, and the caregiver can write it down. Together they'll create a book written by the child! In this way, you're inviting the children to make up stories and encouraging family engagement.

 A WORD FROM THE EXPERT   MARI NOWITZ

▪ Reading and Interactivity

There are so many ways to sneak interactive bits into reading with a group of kids. One of my favorite ways of making a story interactive is to ask my storytime kids about what is happening in the book. I particularly enjoy finding out what the kids think about how the characters are feeling. It gives me a little window into the way these kids I spend time with each week think and feel.

I love books that are songs. If the song is familiar or easy to teach, books that are songs are automatically interactive, because the kids sing them with me. Rhyming books are also fabulous for creating moments of interaction. It is so much fun to leave off the end rhymes as I'm reading so that the children can say the words themselves. Their eyes get so interested and sparkly when they realize they know what word comes next in the story!

I enjoy evaluating stories to figure out how to insert interactive techniques, but sometimes it is a nice break to use books that have interaction built in, like *Rhyming Dust Bunnies*, by Jan Thomas.[14] The questions that make the story interactive are right there for you to read, and the kids get to shout out all the answers, which they love.

I highly recommend watching other storytime presenters to learn new interactivity ideas. One of my favorites, from my colleague Sara Lachman, is to use repeated words in a story as a way of getting the kids to participate. When a book repeats a word or phrase, you can prepare the kids ahead of time so that when you point to that word or phrase, they get to all say it together. It's amazing how fun it is for them, and for me as well.

■ Tips for Reading

When choosing books for storytime, I specifically search out ones that have an interactive element. Interactivity means fun for everyone—for me and for the kids. Plus, interactivity gives me an automatic reminder to do a quick literacy tip for the adults in the room. I want to make sure that parents and caregivers know that what we do when sharing stories is great for their children.

■ Reading with Different Age Groups

With preschool storytime, I think a lot about the way that the kids will interact with the books that I'm reading. I especially enjoy questions that get at what they understand about the story and questions that help them connect with the characters. I also love asking, "What do you think is going to happen?" Watching kids learn to make predictions is so much fun!

Another thing I like to do with preschool age groups is to incorporate activities that have a reading focus. For instance, I have laminated cards for a game I call "word smushing." Each card has a simple word and a picture. (Some examples are *key, pit, bat*, etc.) I choose three each week to share with the children. We look at the cards together and say each word. Then I place them on our flannelboard. First we say the words slowly in the order I have them on the board. Then we smush them together on the count of three, as if we were sounding out a long and interesting word. "One, two, three—keypitbat!" Of course, the word we come up with sounds ridiculous, and we all laugh about it before saying it again. Kids who are farther along in learning to read get a chance to see and recognize short words, and also get a feeling for what sounding out longer words will be like when they start to read. Even prereaders can join in, since they can "read" the pictures.

At least once during the storytime session, even for my baby storytimes, I'll read a book I've chosen specifically because it will be funny and appealing to the grown-ups. The kids of course will like it, too, but I want the parents and caregivers to know that there are lots of books available that have humor that they will enjoy as much as—or maybe even more than—their children will. I remind the caregivers that if they share books they love with their children, their children will learn to love reading.

■ How to Share with Parents about Reading

Over the last few years, I've come to *love* giving parents and caregivers literacy tips during storytime. I didn't always feel that way, though! I remember being exposed to the first Every Child Ready to Read, and feeling so awkward each time I tried to talk directly with the adults in the room about early literacy. Some of my attitude change is due to practice, and forcing myself through the awkwardness toward feeling more comfortable with the material. The more I read and learn about what is happening when kids are learning, the more excited I am to share what I know with our patrons who are parents. Plus, now that I can point to the VIEWS2 research, I feel even more confident that what we do together in storytime really makes a difference for the kids in my community. Now when I share a literacy tip, I feel like a cheerleader. I'm getting to show our parents all of the fabulous things they can do for their kids while playing, reading, and having fun together!

When I share literacy tips in storytime, I try to make them short and direct, talking specifically about what we are doing and how it helps children learn. Recently, I've added another layer. I occasionally let my storytime adults know that I spend a lot of time thinking, reading, and being trained in early literacy topics to better understand why early literacy is so important for our children. I'll let them know that if they want to know more, they can talk to me whenever they have time.

I actually have had people come to me afterward and say, "You know, that's really interesting. Tell me more." During one storytime session, I had enough people who were interested in learning more that I designed a couple of e-mails with links to online early literacy sites to explore. The parents and caregivers were very appreciative, and I had the chance to expose them to so much more information than I can fit into my quick weekly tips.

Sharing an early literacy tip is now something I can't imagine doing without. I intentionally take time just before storytime to make sure I have clear in my mind the tip I want to share that day. While I enjoy this part of storytime for any age, I particularly appreciate when I get to share literacy tips with parents of infants. Because infants are often calm and happy being cuddled in a grown-up's lap during storytime, I feel I have a little more time and flexibility. I can go into a little more detail about early literacy without the kids getting restless, as toddlers or preschoolers might. I love that I get that time with the parents while their kids are so small. They are just starting their parenting adventures, and the fact that each week I have the opportunity to share my enthusiasm around reading, books, and early literacy feels like a gift and an honor.

READING AND SCAFFOLDING

Reading offers numerous opportunities to support early literacy not only because books are so rich in language, but also because they offer the opportunity for children to learn about things outside their own experiences and to stretch their imaginations. Reading and talking overlap—we have seen in chapter 2, "Talking," how we can expand books through the way we talk and encourage children to talk.

In general, the youngest children respond to pictures with stark contrast and bright colors, then with more detail in the illustrations and ones that can be easily labeled, where the words are more concrete. However, we want even the youngest children to be exposed to all kinds of words so it is important to use the book as a jumping-off point for more words. Preschoolers are able to understand more imaginative stories and will often make up their own stories. The older the child, the more intricate the plot can be. However, children will be able to understand more complicated plots in one-on-one book sharing than in groups. Remember, when children are infants, every word you say is new, so they are learning new words from all of your talking and reading. As children get older and are speaking, they are using words they already know. Just having them talk is not necessarily developing their vocabulary unless you are adding to it, like including description or introducing new words.

Let's look here at one decoding component—print awareness—and one comprehension component—vocabulary—to see how we might scaffold these as part of sharing books in storytime.

Print Awareness

- **With children ages birth to 18 months**. Print awareness includes knowing how to handle a book and understanding that pictures and words carry meaning. When babies chew on a book, they are exploring what a book is like. When they seem to be batting or hitting the book, they are trying to imitate your turning the pages, but they do not yet have the coordination to do so. For babies, we point to the pictures and label the object or describe what is happening. Toddlers become more adapt at turning thick pages and will point to pictures themselves, allowing you to say what it is and to describe what is happening. It is important for toddlers to know that the picture represents the real thing, so it is helpful if you can, bring in the real item or a prop for them to see the connection between the two-dimensional object in the book and the three-dimensional object.
- **With children ages 18 to 36 months**. Print awareness for this age group is growing; they not only learn how to turn thick pages in a board book but also the paper pages as their coordination improves. They also know when a book is upside down and will turn it the right way. Running your finger under the text for the title of the book helps them understand that we are reading the text, not the pictures, though pictures can help us understand the story and even add to what is in the text. You can also point out text in the pictures of the book. Children may have a favorite character and are beginning to understand how stories work, anticipating what might come next.
- **With children ages 36 to 60 months**. Print awareness for these children includes knowing the title, the author, and the illustrator of the book and what roles they play. As the children say a repeated phrase, point to the words in the rhythm that they say them so they get the sense they are reading. You may help them identify a word before starting the story.

Vocabulary

- **With children ages birth to 18 months**. Vocabulary for this age group develops quickly. For infants, simply talking about the items in a book and adding more information or a story to each picture helps them build vocabulary. Pointing to a picture as you say the words helps them make sense of what you are saying. Use the book as a conversation starter. Even if there are only one or two pictures or words on a page, talk about the pictures; add information or use the pictures as a jumping-off point for a memory or a story. They need to hear many words and many repetitions to learn.

  In storytimes, role playing with a doll how to share books with babies helps parents/caregivers envision how they can share books with the youngest children. Then you can offer an opportunity for caregivers to share books with their children at the end of storytime by having enough board books for each family for a "read-together time."
- **With children ages 18 to 36 months**. Some books with simple plots use simple vocabulary. You can enrich the vocabulary of this age group by offering a less-familiar word as a synonym. Other books with simple plots have quite

interesting vocabulary with unfamiliar words. In that case you can take time to explain a word or say a more familiar synonym. There is no need to explain every single unfamiliar word if the children are getting the idea of the story. Some explanation can take place before or after you have shared the book.

▪ **With Children Ages 36 to 60 Months.** Use a book as an opportunity to talk about two similar words and what they mean with this age group. For example, in *Llama Llama Red Pajama*, by Anna Dewdney,[15] the baby llama whimpers, weeps, and wails. These are all words related to crying. How are they similar? Different? You might not interrupt the story for this discussion, but you could have the children demonstrate these different kinds of crying and describe them. Many books will not have the synonyms stated right in the book, but you can provide a synonym and discuss similarities and differences in the meanings of two words.

Reading aloud to children is the single most important activity for building knowledge for their eventual success.[16] Sharing books with children adds another dimension to talking. Books can expose children and their parents or caregivers to experiences they've never had, and can offer information to children that they and their parents or caregivers do not know. While adding a richness to language that conversational talk does not offer, books are a window to the world.

NOTES

1. Mari Nowitz is a youth services librarian who firmly believes you can never have enough pairs of crazy socks. She loves almost everything she gets to do as a part of her work at the Tumwater (Washington) Timberland Library, but storytime is almost always the highlight of her week.

2. William H. Teale, "Public Libraries and Emergent Literacy: Helping Set the Foundation for School Success," in *Achieving School Readiness: Public Libraries and National Education Goal*, vol. 1 (Chicago: American Library Association, 1995), p. 118.

3. D. S. Arnold and Grover J. Whitehurst, "Accelerating Language Development Through Picture Book Reading: A Summary of Dialogic Reading and Its Effect," in *Bridges to Literacy: Approaches to Supporting Child and Family Literacy*, ed. David K. Dickinson (Cambridge, MA: Blackwell, 1994), 103–28; A. A. Zevenbergen and Grover J. Whitehurst, "Dialogic Reading: A Shared Picture Book Reading Intervention for Preschoolers," in *On Reading Books to Children: Parents and Teachers*, ed. A. vanKleeck, S. A. Stahl, and E. B. Bauer (Mahwah, NJ: Erlbaum, 2003), 177–200.

4. Grover J. Whitehurst, "Dialogic Reading: An Effective Way to Read to Preschoolers," *Reading Rockets*, accessed June 18, 2015, www.readingrockets.org/article/dialogic-reading-effective-way-read-preschoolers.

5. Aftab Opel, Syeda Saadia Ameer, and Frances E. Aboud, "The Effect of Preschool Dialogic Reading on Vocabulary among Rural Bangladeshi Children," *International Journal of Educational Research* 48, no. 1 (2009): 12–20, doi:10.1016/j.ijer.2009.02.008.

6. Whitehurst, "Dialogic Reading."

7. Kate McMullan, *I Stink!*, illus. Jim McMullan (New York: Joanna Cotler Books, 2002).

8. Jill M. Pentimonti, Laura M. Justice, and Shayne B. Piasta, "Sharing Books with Children," In *Early Childhood Literacy: The National Early Literacy Panel and Beyond*, ed. Timothy Shanahan and Christopher J. Lonigan (Baltimore: Paul H. Brookes, 2013), 117–34; Laura M. Justice and Helen K. Ezell, "Print Referencing: An Emergent Literacy Enhancement Strategy and Its Clinical Applications," *Language, Speech & Hearing Services in Schools* 35, no. 2 (2004): 185–93.

9. Public Library Association (PLA) and Association for Library Services to Children (ALSC), "Every Child Ready to Read @ Your Library—2nd Edition," 2011, www.everychildreadytoread.org/.

10. Bonny Becker, *A Visitor for Bear*, illus. Kady MacDonald Denton (Cambridge, MA: Candlewick Press, 2008).

11. Karma Wilson and Jane Chapman, *Bear Says Thanks* (New York: Margaret K. McElderry Books, 2012).

12. Denise Fleming, *In the Small, Small Pond*, illus. by the author (New York: Henry Holt, 1993).

13. Maurice Sendak, *Where the Wild Things Are*, illus. by the author (New York: Harper & Row, 1963).

14. Jan Thomas, *Rhyming Dust Bunnies*, illus. by the author (New York: Atheneum Books for Young Readers, 2009).

15. Anna Dewdney, *Llama Llama Red Pajama*, illus. by the author (New York: Viking, 2005).

16. R. C. Anderson, E. H. Hiebert, J. A. Scott, and I. A. G. Wilkinson, *Becoming a Nation of Readers: The Report of the Commission on Reading* (Washington, DC: The National Institute of Education, 1984).

WORKSHEET

Reflection Questions on Reading

1. What is the target age group of my storytimes?

   _____

2. What age groups actually attend my storytimes?

   _____

3. How do I model reading to fit the age group(s) of children who attend my storytimes, using behaviors from the VPT?

   _____

   _____

4. How have I been successful in doing so?

   _____

   _____

5. How do I model interactivity to encourage children to participate in reading during my storytime?

   _____

   _____

6. How have I been successful in doing so?

   _____

   _____

7. How do I practice dialogic reading during storytime?

   _____

   _____

8. How do I scaffold reading activities for different ages and abilities in my storytime?

   _____

   _____

9. How do I talk with parents/caregivers about reading with their child(ren)?

   _____

   _____

10. What would I change for a future storytime to incorporate behaviors around reading interactively in my storytime?

    _____

    _____

11. How do I incorporate fun into my reading activities?

    _____

    _____

SINGING

I couldn't do storytime without singing and songs. It would be boring. Singing just makes it fun and makes the flow of storytime go better. Singing breaks down everyone's inhibitions. Even with the child who is just sitting there and doesn't want to participate, when you start singing, they want to join in.

—Gailene Hooper, Supervising Librarian, Republic Public Library[1]

"ITSY BITSY SPIDER," "ROW, ROW, ROW YOUR BOAT," AND** "Twinkle, Twinkle, Little Star" are just a few of the songs traditionally included in storytimes. The repetitive words and simple gestures enable children to learn the songs quickly and join in, thereby participating in a social activity, moving their bodies to build gross and fine motor skills, reinforcing vocabulary, and learning about rhythm and rhyme. Songs are easy for children to learn and memorize, helping to build their memorization and listening skills. Incorporate some shorter songs that include rhyming words and have a strong rhythm, as these songs are easier for children to memorize.[2]

Singing in storytime can include basic songs, songs with gross motor movement, fingerplays set to song, and sing-along books. One consistent element of storytime that lends itself to singing is the opening and closing routine. These times are the perfect place to include the same song (perhaps with movement) every week. This way the children memorize the songs and they recognize the song as an indicator that storytime is beginning and ending. During storytime, you can use fingerplays set to song and sing-along books to break up the book reading and add more interest. Songs with movement are great to use after you finish a book, when the children have been sitting for a bit, to allow the children to get up and move. Singing familiar songs fast or slow, loud or soft brings out different aspects of the songs and makes them exciting and fun. You can also emphasize rhythm and parts of a word by clapping along to the beat and the syllables.

IMPERFECT PITCH!

Be sure to tell parents and caregivers that they don't have to be great singers either. Their children will love hearing them sing songs, and this activity will help teach the children about rhyme and meter, whether or not the tune is pitch perfect!

Whether you are singing a song, singing with a fingerplay, or reading a sing-along book, keep in mind that you don't have to be a great singer. You don't even necessarily have to carry a tune. Do your best and the children will learn the songs as they sing with you. In addition, don't worry about trying to include new and different songs every week. Repeating songs from week to week means that the children will be able to memorize the songs and will look forward to them. Singing is a great way to include everyone—even the adults—in the storytime fun!

WHY IS SINGING IMPORTANT?

Singing has been an important part of storytimes for several decades. Initially, singing may have been included in storytime just because it entertains and engages children. However, we now know that singing is a crucial activity for language and learning skills. More and more research has demonstrated that music and singing contributes to young children's learning and brain development. Researchers have found that singing and music activate the entire brain in different ways and can create new pathways in children's brains.[3] A study done in 2003 measured cortisol levels to determine connections between maternal singing and interest levels in infants.[4]

Singing emphasizes many early literacy practices, and it contributes to oral language development by slowing down language and making it easier for the children to hear the words. Because children are encouraged and want to join in, singing provides them with the opportunity to practice speaking the words and phrases in the song.[5] The slowing down of the language in a song also supports phonological awareness, making children more aware of the sounds of the words, which can help children break down the sounds in words and start to recognize individual letter sounds.[6] This helps prepare children to decode print. Singing is also an incredibly powerful way to increase children's vocabulary—storytime songs include many new and uncommon words that the children are learning as they memorize the song.[7]

Singing also contributes to many skills that are crucial for early learning. Putting words and information to melody helps children to learn and recall content.[8] Learning songs also helps build memorization and listening skills in children. Incorporating body and finger movements with songs encourages gross and fine motor skills, rhythm, and spatial awareness. Singing and songs also help ease the transition from one activity to another, which is why opening and closing songs can be so important for storytime.[9] Overall, singing is a fun and inviting way to engage all children in storytime while supporting their learning and brain development.

VPT AND SINGING IN STORYTIMES: HOW DO I DO IT?

As with talking and reading, singing is a natural part of storytime for every age. There are countless resources with countless songs to choose from for nearly any topic and learning area. Many of us remember the songs we grew up with, and we want to pass those on to our children. And that tradition is important. As a matter of fact, passing on those songs and sharing new ones also helps build children's literacy development.

Touching on aspects of every domain in the VPT, singing also enables you to pause for interaction and responses from your young audience; we encourage your songs to be as interactive as they can be. Finishing the end of a rhyme, shouting out a repeated phrase, everyone singing together including the parents—these are all excellent ways to help make singing a part of children's early literacy development. In many ways, talking and singing have similar goals, and you may notice some overlap in this chapter.

Communication

Singing is a kind of communication, using rhyme, meter, and rhythm to share an idea. With even the youngest child, singing can be incredibly effective in capturing attention and presenting information or sharing a story.

> *Good morning, good morning!*
> *How are you today?*
> *We're here together at storytime.*
> *Hooray, hooray, hooray!*

A simple song such as this one brings children together, identifies the space and the activity in which they are participating, and communicates the upbeat, playful mood of the activity. What songs do you share in your openings and closings to communicate with your children?

Look at the VPT under the domain of Communication:

- **With children ages birth to 18 months,** the nonverbal greetings you use—such as waving hello—can be part of an opening song, communicating what is taking place both through those gestures and through your song. Using your hands as you sing to illustrate some of the words is a good way of capturing little ones' attention.
- **With children ages 18 to 36 months,** you can incorporate songs into your storytimes that use animal noises or onomatopoetic words, communicating how sound effects can be used to convey meaning. Did you know that you're modeling for children how they can use sound effects in their own play, and in the songs they make up for themselves? These kinds of songs are excellent opportunities for varied meter, too—sing them super fast or really slowly to be extra silly and to teach children about rhythm.
- **With children ages 36 to 60 months,** often those in this age group can get wriggly in a storytime. By using a song to encourage good listening, you're providing valuable feedback and positive reinforcement for the children to listen and pay attention. Similarly, you're modeling for the parents that they can use singing in their everyday interactions with their children. Clapping can be part of your method here, too.

I remember all of the songs that I learned as a child—and they stuck in my mind. Singing is really important for memorization, memories, and feeling good about learning. I know that singing connects neuro-pathways. It builds memory and gives them a strong sense of rhythm and helps them to be better able to understand and produce language; even patterns and problem solving [are involved].

—Gailene Hooper

Language Use

As you've seen in previous chapters, language use, or how we use words, fits across many of these practices and across the literacy domains. With singing in particular, language can be used to share a thought or a story in a song or a chant. Some songs can even incorporate taking turns, enabling a conversation between you and the children in your storytime. "BINGO," for instance, invites children to clap in place of syllables, teaching how language can be used or even replaced by sounds.

Look at the VPT under the domain of Language Use:

- **With children ages birth to 18 months,** you can choose very simple nursery rhymes that have a singsong or chant aspect to them and highlight certain easy words for the children to point out. For instance, in "Rain, Rain, Go Away," you can focus on the word *rain* and perhaps even have a prop of a cutout raindrop. In this way, you're encouraging your little ones to listen to oral stories and point out individual, simple words to use on their own.
- **With children ages 18 to 36 months,** fingerplays are excellent for encouraging active movement during a song. "Itsy Bitsy Spider" or "Hickory Dickory Dock" are brief stories, when you think about it, and incorporate small and large actions that build motor movement and enable children to use their hands while speaking.
- **With children ages 36 to 60 months,** you can encourage these older ones to ask questions and think about details by singing a song such as "I Know an Old Lady Who Swallowed a Fly." Props are always a great way to prompt memory and provide visual reinforcement. The children can begin to develop critical thinking skills and learn to hold a longer story in their head.

Phonological Awareness

This domain is perhaps most pertinent to singing because of its emphasis on the sounds of letters and words. Singing as an activity slows down language to a syllabic level, enabling you and the children to think about and hear the sounds that make up the words in a song. Even a song as simple as the alphabet song, when sung too quickly, can seem simply a collection of random sounds and syllables rather than distinguishable letter sounds. Take the time to sing songs slowly and then quickly, and think about focusing on rhyming sounds to help the children learn about language.

Look at the VPT under the domain of Phonological Awareness:

- **With children ages birth to 18 months,** choose books that have few words and lots of rhymes so that you can encourage the children to fill in the rhyming words as you go. Try singing all the words—you can make up your own tune. The singing will help cue the children when it's time to join in. You may need to model this a few times, but if you read the same book often, your little ones will catch on and recite the last word of familiar rhymes, with assistance.

- **With children ages 18 to 36 months,** you can actually do the same activity, perhaps with less assistance and with more complex songs—here, too, "I Know an Old Lady" can be an excellent choice. In fact, you could change things up even with an easy song by choosing different words for ending rhymes. In "Row, Row, Row Your Boat," you can end with "beam" instead of "dream."
- **With children ages 36 to 60 months,** think about the beginning word sounds in the songs you choose. When you sing "Old MacDonald," for instance, you can emphasize the sound of the *c* in "cow" and the *m* in "moo," encouraging the children to think about how the words they're singing actually sound in relation to how they're spelled. Another fun song to think about word sounds is "Apples and Bananas," in which you replace the *a* in "apples" with first an *e*, then an *i*, then an *o*, and so on—same thing with the *a* sound in "bananas."

Vocabulary

Children's songs are full of words, easy and difficult, that can expand a child's vocabulary. Better still, the fact that the words are set to music and have a rhythm might actually help the children remember the word. You can take a moment in your singing to talk about the words you're using if some of them are unfamiliar, so that the children can come away with some new words to try out at home.

Singing songs in other languages is a wonderful way of expanding a child's vocabulary and taking a moment to share these new words. Similarly, incorporating American Sign Language into a song enables children to think about the words they know and how they would express them differently using their hands.

Look at the VPT under the domain of Vocabulary:

> Singing is also super rich in vocabulary. There are always words in songs that you never hear anywhere else.
> —Gailene Hooper

- **With children ages birth to 18 months,** here again you'll see the use of gestures as part of developing vocabulary for young children and helping them learn to communicate. You can also invite children to identify objects on a flannelboard if you use one as part of your song, or shouting out the words when you get to a particular part of the song. Encourage parents to participate in this and say the words to their babies.
- **With children ages 18 to 36 months,** singing can overlap here with talking, and so in your songs you can introduce unfamiliar words or ask children what they think a word means. Repetition is key here; sing an unfamiliar song many times throughout your storytimes and you'll help children learn new words to use on their own. "Jack and Jill" uses the word "crown" as the soft part of the head rather than the headdress of royalty and can be a learning opportunity. You could encourage the children to touch their heads when they sing the word "crown" to reinforce the concept.
- **With children ages 36 to 60 months,** you can sing "Head, Shoulders, Knees, and Toes" but substitute other body parts to see if those words still rhyme, or do the actions in a different order to prompt children to think about the song sequentially. Ask children, "What do we do next?" They love being the experts! Good sequencing songs are "The Hokey-Pokey," "Green Grass Grows All Around," and other cumulative songs.

Comprehension

Some songs are simple and straightforward and might seem as though they don't necessarily require comprehension. Other songs, such as "Five Little Monkeys," require children to follow the number sequence and perhaps even think a little bit about why the doctor keeps saying, "No more monkeys jumping on the bed!" You can deepen their comprehension by taking a moment to ask children about the songs they're singing and the fingerplays they're doing. You can help them start to develop those critical thinking skills here, too. Why is the spider in "Itsy Bitsy Spider" washed out by the rain? And why do you think it decides to climb that spout again?

Look at the VPT under the domain of Comprehension:

- **With children ages birth to 18 months,** you can sing songs that have simple questions in them, such as "Where Is Thumbkin?" Or you can sing a song like "A-Tisket, A-Tasket" multiple times and ask the children to pick different colors to sing each time. You're helping them to pay attention to the song, respond appropriately to familiar words, and follow directions.
- **With children ages 18 to 36 months,** think about ways you can encourage them to share their experiences with the songs you sing in your storytime. You can sing "Wheels on the Bus" and either beforehand or afterward ask them to raise their hands if they've ridden on a bus, if they went up and down on the bus, if they put money in, if the wipers went swish, swish, swish. The children can share their experiences and make the song more real for themselves that way.
- **With children ages 36 to 60 months,** you can talk about real and made-up words, and so the song "Apples and Bananas" can work here, too, as you focus on what words sound like and whether they're real words or silly words.

Print Concepts

When you think about singing and print concepts, it's helpful to think about songs that tell a story. Once again, "I Know an Old Lady" presents a multitude of opportunities to think about characters, objects, experiences, and more. "The Bear Went Over the Mountain," "I Went Walking," "Down by the Bay," "Five Green and Speckled Frogs"—these all present opportunities to include a flannelboard and give the children objects to point to and relate to the song as you all sing together. After you hand out a flannelboard piece to each child, they come forward to put the piece on the flannelboard, making the connection to the word (you can always have more than one piece of an object so that all the children can be included). Books that feature songs are optimal for this domain, too.

Look at the VPT under the domain of Print Concepts:

- **With children ages birth to 18 months,** you can read sing-along books that enable you to talk about what's happening in the pictures and sing the song. There are many of this kind of book to choose from, in both paperback and board book format for very little ones. Using books will help the children in your storytime learn to pay attention to pictures and words in print while also listening to a song.

- **With children ages 18 to 36 months,** you can touch on emotions and emotional experiences of characters in stories by interjecting quick questions as you sing a song like "Five Little Ducks": "How do you think the little ducks feel when they get lost? How does Mama Duck feel when all her ducklings are gone? And then do you think Mama Duck is happy or sad when her little ones come back with presents for her?"
- **With children ages 36 to 60 months,** you can sing "BINGO" and focus on the letters of the word as they disappear throughout the song. You may want a flannelboard here, too; ask the children to identify the letters that remain and even the letters that have been taken away.

Alphabetic Knowledge

Singing and letters might lead you to immediately think of the alphabet song—and that's a good one to incorporate from time to time. You can play with tempo and volume when you sing it to keep it fresh and fun. But there are other opportunities to explore with letters when singing. Having a surface to display letters—such as a flannelboard, whiteboard, or digital device—will help with including alphabetic knowledge in singing a variety of songs.

Look at the VPT under the domain of Alphabetic Knowledge:

- **With children ages birth to 18 months,** you can sing a song that has repeated sounds, such as "Old MacDonald" and have the children imitate the sounds, such as "ee-i-ee-i-o."
- **With children ages 18 to 36 months,** you can use the tune of the song "BINGO" but substitute any five-letter word, such as *PIZZA* or *PUPPY*. Encourage the children to sing the letters with you while you are putting the letters on a flannelboard, whiteboard, or a digital device. Before or after the song, introduce the idea that these are letters and that they make up words.
- **With children ages 36 to 60 months,** with any song you sing, you can emphasize letters or words by placing the letters of an emphasized or repetitive word on a flannelboard, whiteboard, or a digital device. When you sing the word, point to it; if it suits the song, sing the letters individually while pointing to each one. Another idea is to sing the alphabet to the tune of "Mary Had a Little Lamb."

Writing Concepts

We bet you're thinking that writing and singing can't possibly go together. In fact, it's quite possible to write in the air or on babies' bellies during a song and thereby find clever ways of incorporating writing into storytime, even in relatively large groups.

Remember, too, that you can provide prereading activities that involve grasping, pinching, pointing—all of which use muscles that will help with later writing activities. So fingerplays and movement activities are excellent opportunities to build these prewriting muscles.

Look at the VPT under the domain of Writing Concepts:

- **With children ages birth to 18 months,** you can sing "Itsy Bitsy Spider" multiple times and really focus on helping children make those gross motor movements that go along with the song. Encourage parents to model the motions and help their children. You can also focus on the letter *s* here and how it appears many times in the song; encouraging the parents to help the children to make an *s* in the air with their hand or a finger whenever they sing the *s* sound.
- **With children ages 18 to 36 months,** you can sing "The Hokey-Pokey" and suggest that they draw a letter with their feet as part of the song—perhaps instead of shaking it all about. This gross motor movement helps children develop their muscles and is also a fun, silly way to try writing.
- **With children ages 36 to 60 months,** you encourage drawing in the air with the older children, too, perhaps drawing shapes as well as letters. When you sing "Round Is a Pancake," have the children draw a circle each time you say, "Round is a. . . ." This helps children understand that the shapes they're drawing in the air represent real objects, just as the shapes of letters represent real letters.

A WORD FROM THE EXPERT — GAILENE HOOPER

We do "Rum Sum Sum" every week. I've heard that a parent once said that when they drove by the library, the baby started going, "Rum, sum, sum. Rum, sum, sum." He related that with just driving by the library.

■ Singing and Interactivity
Each week I use a manipulative object, perhaps a parachute or scarves, shakers, or sticks for tapping. I also really like to reinforce classic nursery rhymes and songs. I have a collection of props, like fox finger puppets and butterfly nets. And we do "A-hunting we will go, a-hunting we will go, catch a fox and put him in a box, and then we'll let him go." I'm using tools or creating tools that allow children to experience the song. You see it with your eyes and you experience doing it and you're singing it. It really makes lots of neuro-pathways go zinging all over the place for sure.

■ Tips for Singing
When children come in, I like to introduce them to one another. We clap their names and say them really loud and then really soft. We break down their names into syllables. And we're doing the same ones over and over, so that helps with memorization. Then we also do "Rum Sum Sum," with clapping and singing. And we do it really loud, and we do it regular, and then really loud, and then really soft so we're not even saying anything. It settles the children down and it gets them really quiet. They're ready for a story.

So I use singing as an introduction. Sometimes we'll change. Instead of "Hickety-Pickety Bumblebee," we'll do the ABC song on a regular basis, which is a song they already know. We do that a lot—the ABC song is something that we all learned when we were children. And we still remember it. It's engrained in our brain.

VIEWS2 has strengthened a lot of what I do for sure. Sometimes you just think, "Why do I do that?" You just do it and do it and you don't really think about it. It was fun instead to think, "Yes, this is what I do and I know why I do it."

—Gailene Hooper

Then I use books that are songs. There are many, many books out there that have singing in them. Almost every song, from "Itsy Bitsy Spider" and "Row, Row, Row Your Boat" to some [other] basic and simple ones like "There's a Hole in Your Bucket"; I have a collection of probably twenty-five to thirty books, including *The Spooky Wheels on the Bus*.[10] I choose those because they really pull the kids in, especially if they're starting to get wiggly or whatever. You start singing in a book and they're all involved. And they're participating because they're singing.

Also, in between the books, I try to come up with songs or action songs that go along with the theme I'm using that week. So as I'm doing my storytimes, I will start with a couple of short books and then we'll do a song or a fingerplay or a nursery rhyme. A lot of the nursery rhymes [can be] songs, too.

Then we do a longer story and then an action song of some kind, or maybe [we] use shakers or musical instruments or parachutes or something else to go along with that. And then every week we have the same goodbye song. We do "See You Later, Alligator," and I've laminated pictures of each of the things we're singing about. There's a picture of an alligator, a crocodile, and a jellyfish and other animals. As they leave, we sing the song. We do the actions, the movements, and then our storytime is over.

▪ Singing with Different Size Groups

If I have a little bit smaller group or a younger group, we'll do "Bluebird, Bluebird." And everybody will get a flannel board bird that they can go up and put on the board to show the different colors. Then we'll sing the different colors.

With a bigger group, I might not do that as much. I might hand out paper birds and everybody can just keep theirs and take it home with them. That way they're not getting up and down as much and there's not as much confusion with a bigger group. And I will definitely incorporate songs that I know the littler ones can participate in, but I don't really worry so much because those little guys who come every week next year will be the bigger guys who know all the songs. So even if they don't participate so much in this year's storytime, they're taking it all in. They're hearing it. Their siblings or older children are singing the songs. So I don't worry too much about the youngest ones.

I do a variety of harder songs and easier songs. But I really try to focus on classics since I know that they're going to be doing extra things in kindergarten. Classics like "Itsy Bitsy Spider" and "Ring Around the Rosey"—the little ones totally enjoy those, and the bigger ones still enjoy them, too.

▪ How to Share with Parents/Caregivers about Singing

First, I mention that singing is a prereading skill. When we're singing, I'll say, "Singing will make it easier for your child to learn how to read." That's pretty basic. But as we're singing, I'll talk about how they learn to memorize things through singing, how they understand how language works by breaking it down into syllables, so that when they learn to read it's easier for them. And I'll talk about language. If we're singing a song like "Curds and Whey," I'll ask, "How many people know what 'curds and whey' is?" Even some parents don't know, so it's definitely a good opportunity to talk about different words that you're not going to hear anywhere else.

Singing helps with developing rich language. Especially with parents, I often do a handout or a color page at the end of storytime. It will have the words to the songs that we've sung that day. And I'll encourage parents, "You know, you can download these onto your MP3 player or your phone."

The nice thing about singing [for caregivers] is that you don't have to be somewhere with a book, with a child on your lap. You can start doing prereading skills just by singing in the car on the way to an event that you're doing or to the grocery store. When you're singing with your child, you're actually preparing them to be ready to read, so I definitely encourage parents to sing with their children. It also helps [parents] to bond with their children. Sometimes it's frustrating, especially with really active children, to sit down and read a book together. But if you start singing, sometimes you're getting the same benefits as reading, but for that little child who's running around and doesn't want to sit down or read a book or listen to it, he can sing "Row, Row, Row Your Boat" while he's running around and it's doing a lot of the same things as reading.

■ **Singing with Technology**

I have an iPad that the library checked out to me. This way, I can actually pull up a song on YouTube if I don't remember the tune. It gives me enough to remember the tune. I just got the iPad and I haven't used it yet in my storytime specifically, but I plan to. In the past what I've done is search for songs on YouTube and then burn them onto a CD in order to use them in my storytime. This way I can just hook the iPad up to my speaker and I can just play the songs. And so, [having the iPad is going to] take a lot less prep time for me. Once I've got [the songs], then I just stick them in the file and they're there [for use in storytime].

SINGING AND SCAFFOLDING

It is important to be aware of some characteristics of songs that make them easier or harder to learn. Songs that are familiar to children are easier than songs that are unfamiliar. Repeating the song a couple of times in [a single] storytime and repeating the song in consecutive storytimes helps the song become familiar.

It can help to have the words to the songs up front, either projected or on a flip-chart. This allows the adults to join in more easily, which encourages the children as well. In addition, you can encourage the adults to sing the songs with their children outside of the library by providing a handout with the words and perhaps a link to the song or tune online with a heads-up that you will be repeating the song the next time.

Using zipper songs, like "Old MacDonald Had a Farm," makes it easy for young children to chime in. In a zipper song, most of the story structure remains the same for all the verses; only a couple of words are changed from verse to verse. The more repetition there is in the song, the easier it is for children to learn it.

Finally, while the children are learning the song, it is good to sing more slowly so they can hear the words and get used to the rhythm. Once they have mastered a song, you can speed up and sing it fast or sing it very slowly, which makes it more challenging but highly entertaining for the children.

Action Songs

Songs with action are perfect to use in storytime because they give the children a chance to move and get their wiggles out. Plus, action songs are a lot of fun and can contribute to the development of gross motor and fine motor skills. While children will typically pick up action songs pretty quickly, it is still important to scaffold the learning for them.

- **With children ages birth to 18 months**. With this type of song, it is easiest for the child when the adult does the action on the baby or with the baby, such as tickling the baby's tummy or lifting the baby high. For example, with "Itsy Bitsy Spider": It is easiest for the child when the adult moves her own fingers up the baby's body like a crawling spider.
- **With children ages 18 to 36 months**. Younger children need to see the song's actions demonstrated first in order to do them, so walk them through the song before singing it. You and the caregiver can demonstrate. With fingerplays, toddlers do best with large motions—whole body, arms, or hands, rather than individual fingers. Once they have the large motions, challenge them to do some of the simpler fine motor motions. For example, with "Itsy Bitsy Spider," have the toddlers start out using large hand motions to represent the spider.
- **With children ages 36 to 60 months**. Preschoolers can be encouraged and challenged to do the action from your words, not your actions. For example, with "Two Little Blackbirds," you might say, "Put up your index finger, your pointer finger." without actually doing the action. Allow children time to internalize what you have said and do the motion. The older children can become the models for the younger children. With fingerplays, challenge your preschoolers to use fine motor and finger motions. For example, with "Itsy Bitsy Spider," children with more dexterity can alternate the thumb and finger for the spider crawling up the waterspout to make the action more of a challenge.

We use singing and music in our storytimes because we have noticed how children, from the cuddled infant to the rowdy preschooler, are drawn to it. Singing and music focuses their attention and gives us yet more opportunities to make those connections between enjoyment and early literacy in child development.

NOTES

1. Gailene Hooper is the supervising librarian at Republic Public Library in Washington State. She is a self-professed book hoarder.
2. Patrick Walton, "Using Singing and Movement to Teach Pre-Reading Skills and Word Reading to Kindergarten Children: An Exploratory Study," *Language and Literacy* 16, no. 3 (2014), available at https://ejournals.library.ualberta.ca/index.php/langandlit/article/view/23441/17341.
3. Valerie L. Trollinger, "The Brain in Singing and Language," *General Music Today* 23, no. 2 (2010): 20–23, doi:10.1177/1048371309353878; F. H. Rauscher, G. L. Shaw, L. J. Levine, E. L. Wright, W. R. Dennis, and R. L. Newcomb, "Music Training Causes Long-Term Enhancement of Preschool Children's Spatial-Temporal Reasoning," *Neurological Research* 19, no. 1 (1997): 2–8.

4. T. Shenfield, S. Trehub, and T. Nakata. "Maternal Singing Modulates Infant Arousal." *Psychology of Music* 31:365–75.

5. Valerie L. Trollinger, "The Brain in Singing and Language," *General Music Today* 23, no. 2 (2010): 20–23, doi:10.1177/1048371309353878.

6. Walton, "Using Singing and Movement."

7. Yvette Coyle and Remei Gómez Gracia, "Using Songs to Enhance L2 Vocabulary Acquisition in Preschool Children," *ELT Journal* 68, no. 3 (2014): 276–85, doi:10.1093/elt/ccu015.

8. Wanda T. Wallace, "Memory for Music: Effect of Melody on Recall of Text," *Journal of Experimental Psychology: Learning, Memory and Cognition* 20, no. 6 (1994): 1471.

9. Sarah Mathews, "Singing Smoothes Classroom Transitions," *Dimensions of Early Childhood* 40, no. 1 (2012): 13–17.

10. J. Elizabeth Mills, *The Spooky Wheels on the Bus*, illus Ben Mantle (New York: Scholastic, 2010).

WORKSHEET

Reflection Questions on Singing

1. What is the target age group of my storytimes?

   _____
   _____

2. What age groups actually attend my storytimes?

   _____
   _____

3. How do I model singing to fit the age group(s) of children who attend my storytimes, using behaviors from the VPT?

   _____
   _____

4. How have I been successful in doing so?

   _____
   _____

5. How do I model interactivity through singing in my storytime?

   _____
   _____

6. How have I been successful in doing so?

   _____
   _____

7. How do I scaffold singing activities for different ages and abilities in my storytime?

   _____
   _____

8. How do I talk with parents/caregivers about singing with their child(ren)?

   _____
   _____

9. What would I change for a future storytime to incorporate behaviors around singing interactively in my storytime?

   _____
   _____
   _____

10. How do I incorporate fun into my singing activities?

   _____
   _____
   _____

PLAYING

~~~~~~~

Play is how children explore the world.

—Susan Anderson-Newham, Early Learning Supervising Librarian,
Pierce County (Washington) Library System[1]

LAY IS AN ESSENTIAL PART OF CHILDHOOD. IT IS CRU-
cial for development and serves as a vehicle for children to engage
in many types of learning. Play is characterized as being motivated
and driven by the child—enjoyable, process oriented, active, and rule governed.[2]
Given that play shares many characteristics with the learning that takes place in
informal learning environments, it is a natural fit for storytimes. Children begin to
integrate and learn new information by playing.

For storytime, we can discuss play in two different ways: structured and unstructured. Structured play typically has specific guidelines and objectives, whereas
unstructured play is open ended, allowing the children to develop their own rules
and guidelines.[3] The specific activities that you include and guide in storytime—like
dancing, bubbles, and parachutes—would fall under structured play. Open playtime
offered before or after storytime, where perhaps you put out a range of toys and let
the children play, would be considered unstructured play. If you have the space and
funding to offer a playtime adjacent to your storytime, we encourage you to do so
because it will allow the children and caregivers time to participate in unstructured
play as well as socialize with each other.

We want to point out that there are certain characteristics of play that can provide
the foundation for your program.

> Play is the perfect
> example of children
> as scientists. They
> explore, experiment,
> and discover things
> about the world and
> each other.
>
> —Susan Anderson-Newham

OBJECTS OR TOYS TO ENCOURAGE DIFFERENT KINDS OF PLAY

- **Functional play**—cars, baby dolls, balls, parachute, books, shapes to sort with
- **Constructive play**—blocks, play dough, writing and art materials, flannelboard with shapes
- **Dramatic play**—puppets, costumes, props

- Activities in your storytime should be play based: interactive, enjoyable, and active.
- Participation in storytime activities should be initiated by the child and supported and scaffolded by you, the storytime provider, and the caregivers.
- As with all the other practices, the support and scaffolding in play should be provided through fun and interactive methods.

There are three types of play that fit well with storytime: functional, constructive, and dramatic.[4] Functional play is essentially when children are playing or exploring with an object, discovering all about it. Active play—when children are using their muscles—can also be considered functional play. Constructive play is the process of making or constructing something. Dramatic play is make-believe or pretend play. All three types of play can be used in structured or unstructured play. With structured play, you have to provide the opportunities for each type in your storytime. However, you probably already offer many activities that support each type of play. You are encouraging functional play when you include movement, like dancing, and items like scarves, bubbles, and shakers. You are encouraging constructive play when you include an opportunity for children to create something. Finally, you are including dramatic play when you have the children pretend or act out something in storytime. With unstructured play, you can support all three types of play just by providing toys or objects that encourage each type of play (see sidebar). Along with the skills and knowledge that children normally acquire from unstructured play, you can also support emergent literacy

THE ROLE OF THE LIBRARIAN IN AN UNSTRUCTURED PLAYTIME

There are three roles that the librarian does during unstructured playtime.

- **A partner**: You play together with somebody if that's what they need at that point. You are a participant following the child's lead.
- **A stage manager:** You set up the room so that it invites play. You put the play dough out on the table with all these little cutters and designs and things. And the children are invited to come play with the play dough.
- **A director:** You think about pushing them up to another level of play. You might ask a question or say, "How about Jane? Why doesn't Jane come and play with Maya? Maybe you two can play together. What else could you add to your building as you play together?" That way either you are helping the children find a new level of play, or you're involving somebody who's not feeling involved.

Through all three roles, you are modeling for the parents the importance of playing and how to play with their children, and you are modeling for the children about how to play. Sometimes you just sit down and you yourself start playing. If it's blocks, you start building. If it's flannelboards, you start dressing them or telling a story. If it's a baby doll, you might rock the baby back and forth or start to feed the baby so that you become like a player and a director.

It's important for librarians to look around the room for opportunities to model playing. When parents and caregivers see the librarian jumping in, they will feel compelled to jump in and play as well.

—SUSAN ANDERSON-NEWHAM

and numeracy skills in unstructured playtime by providing books, writing utensils, letter puzzles, magnetic letters, or dramatic play objects (to encourage oral language and narrative skills).

We are not saying that you have to include every type of play in every storytime. It is more about providing different types of opportunities for play across many storytimes. While we encourage you to include an unstructured playtime before or after your storytime, you do not have to include every type of play in the playtime. Rely on your instincts and knowledge of your community and do what works best for them and your library. Remember that this book is a guide with suggestions for overall effective practices. You, as the storytime provider, have the knowledge and expertise to transform the information in this book into effective practices for your community and library. The main point we want you to take away is that play is an important learning and development process for children, so as an informal learning environment, your library should be encouraging, including, and promoting play.

WHY IS PLAY IMPORTANT?

Play is one of the most significant activities a child will do in his or her childhood. Play allows children the opportunity to try out and test different ideas and behaviors while also gaining information from peers and adults. In the process of play, children can learn important skills that set the stage for later academic and lifelong learning success, including oral language abilities, creativity, problem solving, and social skills.[5] As children engage in many types of play and across many scenarios, they talk with a wide variety of adults and peers, therefore developing their oral language, narrative skills, and vocabulary. Play helps contribute to later learning success, in part, by supporting the development of executive function abilities, which include working memory, self-regulation, and the ability to plan and organize. Executive function abilities are vital for a child's later academic success because they help to control other behaviors that are crucial to learning.[6] During play, children are developing their problem-solving skills when deciding what they want to play and how they want to go about it. They develop their social skills when playing with their peers and working through conflict that occurs during the play. You can emphasize this with parents and talk with them about how play facilitates and encourages conflict resolution and problem solving.

In addition to helping children develop these skills, play also prepares children for later learning success because when they play, they gain important information and knowledge necessary for later academic achievement. According to the ECRR2 Toolkit, "Playing is one of the primary ways young children learn about the world. General knowledge is an important literacy skill that helps children understand books and stories once they begin to read."[7] Play in literacy-enriched environments can also support emergent literacy and skills.[8] Providing objects and opportunities that encourage early literacy skills—such as books, paper and writing/coloring utensils, and dramatic play props—can help to create literacy-enriched environments. Play can also serve as important process for acquiring cultural information. When children play, they have the opportunity to imitate the behaviors of others within

> Play is this rich, imaginative place where children can discover who they are, where they fit, and what the world is like. The toy industry has placed toys in the starring role, but really, play is not about toys at all.
>
> —Susan Anderson-Newham

their culture, therefore learning crucial information about their cultural practices. By playing with diverse groups of adults and peers, they also have the opportunity to be exposed to cultural practices that differ from their own.[9] When you provide an unstructured playtime, you give children the opportunity to mix with people of different cultures and experiences, helping to broaden their cultural knowledge. Most important, remember that because the library is an informal learning environment, we have a responsibility to provide learning experiences that are fun, enjoyable, child initiated, open ended, active, and interactive—and what better way to do that than through play?

VPT AND PLAY IN STORYTIMES: HOW DO I DO IT?

~~~~~~~~

How do we start incorporating play more into storytimes?

—Susan Anderson-Newham

During our data collection for Project VIEWS2, we did not see as many instances of structured or unstructured play in the storytimes we observed, so we are presenting the practical information in this chapter a little differently from previous chapters. Rather than go domain by domain, we present two examples of structured play in storytimes and an extensive unstructured play example from our librarian expert, Susan Anderson-Newham. We then discuss the types of literacy behaviors found in each example of play and how you can extend this into your own storytimes.

Remember: the goal is not to standardize practice—you are going to bring your own creativity to this work and adapt it to fit your community's needs. Focus on the ways you're already incorporating early literacy and early learning concepts, and how you can be more intentional in planning and delivering your storytimes.

STRUCTURED PLAY EXAMPLE 1

Making Pumpkin Pie (Perfect for 18 to 36 months and for 36 to 60 months)

In one storytime we observed, a librarian led the children in a dramatic play activity in which they pretended to make pumpkin pie. She started with picking the pumpkin and cutting off the top, scooping out the seeds, and then cutting up the pumpkin, adding spices, mixing it all together, putting it into a pie dish, and putting it in the oven. She talked about the tools you use when you're making pumpkin pie, and touched on using knives and a hot oven, saying that because this is pretend play, the kids can do these actions themselves, whereas normally they would need an adult to help them. She incorporated sensory elements by encouraging children to imagine what the seeds feel like (a goopy, gooey mess); what the aroma of baking pie smells like (yum); what the finished pie tastes like (yum, yum!). She led the children in many gross motor movements, such as moving their arm in a big circle to mix all the ingredients together; she also counted the number of times she stirred

Scuffles are inevitable during free play, and we encourage librarians to see them as opportunities! A child can't work on conflict resolution skills unless they experience conflict and are guided through it.

When problems arise during play, we can help children discover how to resolve the problem and get along with each other. In essence, play gives children a chance to be unhappy in a safe environment where we bring them back to feeling good; [it helps] them grow socially and emotionally.

—Susan Anderson-Newham

the pie filling. All the way through, the librarian interacted with the children, asking them engaging questions, responding to thoughts and questions from the children, encouraging them to connect this activity with their own experiences. This play pattern embodied several aspects of literacy development, serving as a classic example of the link between early literacy and structured play.

Communication

When we look at the VPT under the domain of Communication, we see that this example presents several opportunities for those behaviors. For instance, the librarian provided pauses both during the activity and when she asked questions, encouraging the children to respond and participate in turn-taking conversations; she prompted children to use adjectives; and she encouraged the use of sound effects during the activity.

Vocabulary

Under the domain of Vocabulary, we can see that the librarian used gestures as well as words to communicate; she presented some unfamiliar vocabulary in the names of the tools she used; she provided experiences about which children could ask questions; and she modeled using multiple words to explain the ideas in the play pattern.

Comprehension

Under the domain of Comprehension, the librarian gave directions and asked simple questions to facilitate each part of the dramatic play; she identified objects and actions by name; and she asked questions that elicited short answers or gestures to demonstrate comprehension.

Writing

Under the domain of Writing, again we see uses of gross motor movements to build those muscles that children need as part of their prewriting development. We also see storytelling, which promotes early writing. Furthermore, if you do this kind of dramatic play, you can talk about shapes—such as the circle you make with your arm when you're mixing—to bring in even more writing-skill development.

This activity is a rich example of how just one activity can make such a difference in presenting a multitude of early literacy behaviors in such an interactive, engaging, and fun way!

STRUCTURED PLAY EXAMPLE 2

Birds (Perfect for Birth to 18 months and 18 to 36 months)

In another storytime we observed, the storytime provider provided an opportunity for exploratory play for babies. For this activity you would need the lyrics to the song "Bluebird, Bluebird" (which can be found online) and a set of bird toys. The bird toys could be stuffed or plastic—just make sure that is safe for babies to play with. Try to have a variety of colors. The storytime provider that we observed had a set of stuffed birds of all different colors that tweet and chirp. Each baby received a stuffed bird to hold and play with while the storytime provider sang "Bluebird, Bluebird." She would sing the song over and over, substituting different colors in the lyrics. When she sang a specific color, she would "fly" her bird over to the babies that had a stuffed bird of that color. She would sing the song until she had completed every color of bird that the babies were holding. While she was singing, the babies were playing with, flying, and manipulating the birds.

A similar activity can be done with older children. For this group, you could use the same bird toys or you could have bird cutouts (perhaps on popsicle sticks). Just try to have some matching birds or birds of the same color. Use the same beginning to the activity as above, with the song and the birds, but as you are singing the song, ask the children who have the color of bird that you are singing about to "fly" their bird around with your bird. Then cycle through all the colors in the song so that everyone has a chance to fly their bird. At the end, you could have the children work to find their bird partners or group—consisting of other children with a matching bird.

Language Use

If you look at the VPT under the domain of Language Use, we can see that the storytime provider used an oral story that included simple ideas (like *bird*) for the babies to begin to associate the name with the item. With toddlers, you could ask them to point to a specific color of bird; or call out a color and have them hold up their matching bird, which helps them learn to identify and locate items that others are talking about.

Phonological Awareness

Under the domain of Phonological Awareness, the song "Bluebird, Bluebird" has so many repetitive phrases that it will quickly become familiar to the children, both babies and toddlers. As a result, you just need to pause and encourage the children to fill in words in the song.

Vocabulary

Under the domain of Vocabulary, we see the storytime provider using many different color words for the babies in the song. If you have older babies, you could prompt them to identify what they are holding. With toddlers, ask them what color birds they are holding as you are singing the song. You could also include some unfamiliar words by mentioning different types of birds that are specific colors or pointing out the bird's body parts, like the wings or beak.

UNSTRUCTURED PLAY EXAMPLE

Story Play Boxes (Pefect for all ages)

We started off by creating what we called "story play times." We constructed themed play boxes with all sorts of items that would invite the children to play; for example, the transportation box had a big floor map (like a road map), vehicles, horses, blocks, and storefronts for building. It also contained large transportation items like stop signs, crossing guard vests, hard hats, and so on. Another example is the travel-themed box that has costumes, passports, and all kinds of other travel-related items. All of the items in these boxes were selected to support the creation of a fun, free play space. We crafted sixteen of these themed boxes. The librarians would reserve and circulate them during a storytime session. They would present their storytime and then open the box and scaffold free play.

When we expanded storytimes to more branches, we simplified the idea and provided every branch with a more generic play box. It contained flannelboard paper dolls with lots of varied clothing; fabric balls; oversized foam dice for rolling, counting, and games; parachutes; a foam bowling set; Tell Me a Story cards; blocks; and play dough.

One interesting discovery was that setting out play dough and blocks *before* storytime was really helpful. It allowed the children and caregivers to transition from the outside world to the library. That ten to fifteen minutes of open-ended activity allowed everyone to be more present for the storytime.

—Susan Anderson-Newham

In Susan's example of play boxes, we see all kinds of unstructured play opportunities prompted by various props. And in the unstructured play, we can see the following examples of literacy behaviors from the VPT.

Communication
We can see examples of how communication is facilitated through taking turns and conversing. For very young children through preschoolers, this kind of unstructured play provides them with the opportunity to use adjectives to describe things and

BLOCK PLAY

One of the easiest ways to begin offering an unstructured playtime is to get a large set of blocks. Include a mixture of big and small and soft and wooden blocks for the different age groups.

> Blocks are amazing because they can become anything. Aside from straight-on building, I've seen children pretend a block was a cell phone and use it to 'text' their friend. I've seen them balance a block on their head as a posture aid, and one time the children spread the blocks out and jumped from block to block, avoiding falling into "hot lava."
>
> **—SUSAN ANDERSON-NEWHAM**

Tips for Block Play from Susan
- Sit down and model building with the blocks and invite everyone to join in, even the parents. If you are enjoying building, the children will imitate you.
- Use open-ended prompts such as "Tell me about this. Tell me what you're doing" when children are building. This helps them start thinking about what they're creating. Most pre-K kids do very little planning when building with blocks; they're just exploring the shapes, aligning and/or stacking. When we talk with them and ask them questions, we are encouraging them to think about what they're doing.
- Work on listening. After an open-ended prompt, really give the children time to think about what you asked so they can answer. Then contemplate how you can build and expand on what they said. (Dialogic block building!)

communicate effectively. By being present during these play sessions and engaging with families, you can model how to respond to children's cues to solicit attention and include pauses so children can respond to questions and tell their stories about their play.

Language Use

Building on communication, this pattern of play further encourages family engagement and language use through storytelling. Children have the opportunity to tell stories about their play and, in so doing, learn to recount events, use words to express thoughts and ideas, begin to follow the sequence of events in an orally narrated story, and further enjoy storytelling. Help them take advantage of these opportunities by playing with them and asking open-ended questions. Engage with the caregivers, too.

Phonological Awareness

Rhythm and rhyme are important parts of literacy development, and play can give children opportunities to use and practice the rhythm and rhyme of language. As the children play with the toys from the play boxes, they may naturally incorporate songs and chants into their play. Playing music as part of playtime, perhaps even to match the theme of playtime, is another way to incorporate the sounds and meter of language into play.

Vocabulary

Play—especially themed play—encourages children to use their words as they narrate their activities and explain them to other children who join in. These are also excellent opportunities to build vocabulary by offering new words for the objects children are playing with, even by bringing in other languages. As the caregivers and storytime providers interact with the children during the playtime, they can ask open-ended questions that encourage existing vocabulary as well as new words that might even be invented words. The earlier example of mitigating and resolving conflict also provides an opportunity to demonstrate how vocabulary is instrumental in the practice of play—children learn how to use the words they need to solve problems.

Comprehension

The themed play boxes in this example enable children to demonstrate comprehension of a particular situation, and how to use the objects in that box. Children learn to identify objects, develop a play activity around one or more of those objects, and have a conversation about their play. Through this process, children build an understanding of how words, stories, directions, and ideas fit together.

Print Concepts

You may have noticed that many of the themed sets included a print piece—the floor map, the passports. These are excellent tools for building print concepts and connections with print. Additionally, you can provide books and other print materials related to a particular theme to enhance the children's connections with books and stories.

Alphabetic Knowledge

The print components also build alphabetic knowledge, through the children's interactions with the print. They can identify an object by the words printed on it; they can also point to certain letters and perhaps distinguish between numbers and letters.

Writing Concepts

While we don't see overt examples of writing activities in this example, we do again see print components included as part of many of the boxes, and we see play opportunities for letter recognition, muscle-building activities, and storytelling, all of which contribute to prewriting skills.

Bottom Line

Play builds preliteracy skills, and offering opportunities for play in your storytimes— whether structured or unstructured—gives children a way to practice what they're learning and gives families a chance to engage.

A WORD FROM THE EXPERT   SUSAN ANDERSON-NEWHAM

■ Playing and Interactivity

In training librarians and teachers, we talk about dialogic reading: we work on asking open-ended questions. When children are building or playing, we'll ask, "Tell me about this" or "Tell me what is happening here."

We also work on not interfering. We might model building, but we don't take over what the child is building. Our job is to ask questions to spur their thinking and support their playing.

We keep Vygotsky's "zone of proximal development" in mind. Think to yourself, how can I move this up a notch? Is there a question I can ask that will spur their thinking and keep the play going? Is there an object I can add that will support further exploration? Can I connect them with another child to enhance the play?

■ Tips for Playing

My whole philosophy about play is that it is discovery. Every caregiver knows that children will choose a real cell phone over a toy cell phone every time! This is because in reality, the toy is simply a colorful object, but the real cell phone seems to have a magical hold on the grown-ups in a child's life. They wonder, what is it? How does it work? How do I make it make that noise? What can I do with it? Why does Mommy use it? What does it feel like to be a grown-up and use this? Providing children the opportunity to play with real objects allows them to explore these sorts of questions, as does open-ended play. When children play, they are investigating how the world works and what it feels like to be a grown-up. They imitate and experiment. They are scientists! So really, our job is to provide them with the opportunity, place, and most important, the time to play.

■ Playing with Different Age Groups

We've always had a playtime after baby time. We present a short and sweet storytime and then pull out a box of balls and dolls and books and manipulatives. We've experimented with different sorts of objects, but the babies tend to find each other most interesting. So we looked for items that would support their interactions with one another. Boxes are wonderful, and bubbles are always popular. We pay attention to the material the toys are made of, since nearly everything gets chewed. And we do a lot of washing of items.

We have been doing Block Parties with preschoolers for a few years now, where we open the unit block cabinets and perhaps add Legos or small blocks. But last year we added Toddler Block to the mix. We purchased large and small foam blocks, and we put out soft balls and durable vehicles and animals. Building on an idea from a colleague, I scanned the small colorful wooden blocks and had the pictures of the blocks glued onto a large span of butcher paper. We laminated this, and it works as a sort of giant matching puzzle—the children grasp a block and look for its match on the paper. Some of the toddlers really enjoy this! And many of the preschoolers will as well.

For preschool, we have the generic play boxes and the story playtime boxes. I also try to look for storytime books that might spark a play idea in the children—another intentional piece of planning. Also, many of our branches will open up the unit block cabinets after preschool storytime. The blocks are a very simple way to add play, since they can become anything. We've also found that our school-age kids love to build with the unit blocks. When some of our branches have Lego programs, they'll open up the block cabinet as well. It's pretty exciting to see what the older children build. They will plan and experiment and create the most amazing structures.

■ How to Share with Parents/Caregivers about Playing

Even though I'm not fond of the "play is children's work" idea, it seems to resonate with parents. I usually emphasize the scientific angle of play. I'll reiterate that fancy toys are not necessary. Rocks, sticks, pots, pans, cardboard boxes—[all] are rich play tools. Plus, real objects around the house. And of course, the very best toy is the parents themselves! I share my support for boredom—it forces imaginative thinking! And I talk to parents about stimulation—exploring the environment, testing, touching, feeling, and smelling. All of this takes time, so I'll also encourage them to give their children lots and lots of free time to play—especially outdoors! If I could redo our libraries, I would create an outdoor space for children to go play and explore, and not necessarily a playground. Big toys and slides are wonderful, but there is nothing quite as open-ended as just exploring an outdoor space with paths and trees and plants—looking for bugs and flowers, checking out rocks with a magnifying glass, lying on your back watching the clouds. These are healthy and rich fodder for the imagination. And they're fun! Who knows? Maybe we'll get funding to add outdoor play spaces someday.

PLAYING AND SCAFFOLDING

With play, it may seem that scaffolding is not as important, but in fact it is just as crucial to scaffold children's play as it is any other practice. We want them to move forward, learn, and continue to develop necessary skills from their play experiences. Children develop play from the more concrete to the more abstract. For example, a younger child will use her own sippy cup, which is empty, to feed a doll. The sippy cup is still a sippy cup but is being used in play. Toddlers often use the toy for the designated purpose, so a truck is used as a truck. An older child may use the truck to represent another object, or they simply imagine the object as they play without having a physical object in hand.

During storytime and playtime, you can provide scaffolding for both structured and unstructured play. However, because the children should guide unstructured play, you don't want to interfere; you only want to support their play. In order to help you see this difference, we have provided an example of scaffolding in structured play and some ways you can scaffold unstructured play.

Structured Play

Let's take the pumpkin pie dramatic play activity described earlier in this chapter. How might we adapt it to different developmental levels?

- **With children ages birth to 18 months**. With this age group, you can definitely do this activity; you just might want to simplify it and take out some of the detail. For babies, use actual props, like a pumpkin, a bowl, and a spoon. Be sure to say the name of each item when holding it up to help build vocabulary. Prompt the caregivers to hold the babies' hands and do the motions with their baby.
- **With children ages 18 to 36 months**. The younger children are, the more concrete their thinking is. For toddlers, again, use real props, like a pumpkin (it would be great if you could have a *real* one!), a bowl, and other items used to make pumpkin pie. All the children can imitate your actions, but the younger ones will comprehend more concretely if you use props. When the children are imitating your actions, keep in mind that younger ones need more time to respond. It is easier for them to follow slower actions, and you may need to repeat the actions and the instructions several times. Prompt the caregivers to do the actions as well, because it will make it easier for the child to see what to imitate. Once the children have mastered the activity, you can add in some pretend items or speed up the activity to make it more challenging.
- **With children ages 36 to 60 months**. With this age group, you do not have to use props because older children can already picture these items and pretend to use them. However, if you want, you could use a mixture of props and pretend items. With preschoolers, you can add in lots of detail, like stirring in specific types of spices and rolling out the crust. At this age, they may still need to imitate your actions; though they may not need as

much repetition, you can demonstrate the actions for them once or twice. Older children can get bored if the motions are too slow, so make things more fun and engaging by starting slowly to mix the ingredients, then speeding it up, while being sure not to spill any out of the bowl. You can also solicit their help with this activity by asking questions, such as "What should we do next?" or "What other ingredients should we add?"

Unstructured Play

Scaffolding unstructured play is a little different from other examples of scaffolding that we have offered. Because unstructured play is directed and driven by the children, you as the adult will want to follow the children's lead. However, because their play may be repetitive, your role is to help them move to a more mature, higher level of play.

Here is an example from Gaye Gronlund's *Developmentally Appropriate Play*:[10]

Two children are pretending to make dinner and ask you if you would like pizza. You say sure and ask them what kind of pizza they have. Then they ask you if you would like something to drink and you ask what they have. After a bit of playing around eating, you find them coming back to the same scenario and asking you again what kind of pizza you would like. This is repetitive play.

To expand their play you may say, "Oh, I'm very full with pizza—what else might you have? Could you make some cookies? What ingredients do we need for cookies? Shall we make a list?" Then you might all pretend to go to the grocery store to buy the ingredients. By asking some simple questions while participating in their play, you have raised the level of play, guiding the children to another scenario with further possibilities.

Learning more about the practice of playing and allowing ourselves the freedom to explore opportunities for structured and unstructured play in storytimes is an exciting development. Play is one of the most important practices for children to engage in to support their learning, and the benefits of play for children and their families is priceless, providing impact for years to come.

NOTES

1. Susan Anderson-Newham is the Early Learning Supervising Librarian for the Pierce County (Washington) Library System, where she manages a large collection of materials and presents trainings on early learning for parents and teachers. She has a BA in developmental psychology and a master's in library and information science. Susan is also a professional storyteller and the author of the book *Cooking Up a Storytime: Mix-and-Match Menus for Easy Programming* (Chicago: ALA Editions, 2014).
2. J. P. Isenberg and N. Quisenberry, "Play: Essential for All Children," position paper of the Association for Childhood Education International, 2002, https://www.acei.org/images/stories/global-action-center/PlayEssential.pdf.

3. Anthony Vecchioni, "Structured vs. Unstructured Play—Is That What Really Matters?", *Spaghetti Box Kids*, September 3, 2008, http://spaghettiboxkids.com/blog/structured-vs -unstructured-play-is-that-what-really-matters/ .

4. Shannon Lockhart, "Play: An Important Tool for Cognitive Development," *HighScope Extensions* 24, no. 3 (2010): 1–8, http://membership.highscope.org/app/issues/142.pdf.

5. Sharon Lynn Kagan, Catherine Scott-Little, and Victoria Stebbins Frelow, "Linking Play to Early Learning and Development Guidelines: Possibility or Polemic?" *Zero to Three (J)* 30, no. 1 (2009): 18–25.

6. Lockhart, "Play: An Important Tool."

7. Association for Library Services to Children (ALSC) and Public Library Association (PLA), *Every Child Ready to Read, 2nd Edition Kit*, 2011, section 1, 5.

8. Kathy Roskos and James F. Christie, "Play in the Context of the New Preschool Basics," in *Play and Literacy in Early Childhood: Research from Multiple Perspectives*, ed. Kathy Roskos and James F. Christie (New York: Routledge, 2009), 83–100.

9. Isenberg and Quisenberry, "Play: Essential for All Children."

10. Gaye Gronlund, *Developmentally Appropriate Play: Guiding Young Children to a Higher Level* (St. Paul, MN: Redleaf Press, 2010).

WORKSHEET

Reflection Questions on Playing

1. What is the target age group of my storytimes?

   _____

2. What age groups actually attend my storytimes?

   _____

3. How do I model playing to fit the age group(s) of children who attend my storytimes, using behaviors from the VPT?

   _____

4. How have I been successful in doing so?

   _____

   _____

5. How do I provide structured and unstructured play activities in my storytimes?

   _____

   _____

6. How do I model interactivity and/or dialogic practices through these types of play activities in my storytime?

   _____

   _____

7. How have I been successful in doing so?

   _____

   _____

8. How do I scaffold play for different ages and abilities in my storytime?

   _____

   _____

9. How do I talk with parents/caregivers about playing with their child(ren)?

   _____

   _____

10. What would I change for a future storytime to incorporate behaviors around playing interactively in my storytime?

    _____

    _____

11. How do I incorporate fun into my playing activities?

    _____

    _____

WRITING

~~~~~~~~

The most important thing about writing is that it conveys information, and if that's going to be the foundation for conveying information, then I think it's very important that even at a young age, kids start to realize what writing is.

—Bonnie Anderson, Children's Librarian, Puyallup (Washington) Public Library[1]

RITING CAN AND SHOULD BE AN IMPORTANT PART OF storytime for children of all ages. Whether we're talking about using actions to support fine motor development, a simple scribble in crayon on a piece of paper, or a block letter–printed name on a tag, exposing children to the act of writing helps them understand that there are many ways to communicate besides talking.[2]

It may seem as if writing can wait until school, where children learn how to correctly write each letter. But in fact, during storytime, you can begin the process of writing readiness by including activities that focus on early writing. Just as reading has early literacy skills to support later reading, writing has "early writing skills" to support later writing. These skills can start out with:

- developing gross and fine motor skills;
- progressing to scribbling and developing an understanding that print is different from pictures and that it communicates an idea;
- identifying letters and writing letter-like shapes; and
- writing actual letters.

Keep in mind that this is a possible progression; all children progress at their own rate and in their own way. Once the children have even just some of these skills, they can use their own "writing" to communicate. This "writing" may be a page covered in scribbles, but if a child scribbles with the intent of expressing a written idea, then she is using early writing skills. The scribbles may just indicate that a child does not yet have the muscle control or the cognitive development to form letters.[3]

In storytime you may also see a natural progression with early writing in children, beginning with scribbling, then progressing to letter-like shapes, followed by actual letters.[4] You can support this progression by providing guidance and opportunities for practice with writing concepts. In particular, you can emphasize print and letter forms in your activities as well as provide children with time to color, make art, and use writing utensils in order to support early writing. In the VPT, you will find behaviors for emphasizing early writing in the domain of Writing Concepts.

Three broad methods for incorporating writing concepts into storytime are:

- name recognition and writing
- storytime activities that support writing
- craft time

Name Recognition and Writing

〜〜〜〜〜

When children are writing their name, they are getting practice with writing, but they're also getting reinforcement in many other early literacy skills because their name is often the first thing that any child will write because that's part of them and it's something that they're going to recognize in whatever context.

—Bonnie Anderson

One particularly meaningful way to introduce writing concepts for preschool children is through their own name. "For many children, names serve as important touchstones to new understandings about letter/sound matches and words."[5] A child's name may serve as the first moment when the child realizes that there is a link between oral language and print.[6] In fact, their own name is typically one of the first words children start to recognize in print and many times is one of the first words they try to write.[7] In storytime you can work on the recognition, spelling, and writing of their names through many activities such as writing or selecting their name tags, activities that emphasize the letters in their names, or having them sign their artwork in craft time.

Storytime Activities That Support Writing Concepts

Including writing concepts in the middle of storytime may not seem to be the most natural fit. However, there are many fun ways to incorporate these concepts—including ways that will be especially useful to those of you who have large storytime numbers or don't have the space for craft time. Any activity that emphasizes print; encourages fine motor development (especially the palmer and pincer grasp); and focuses on shapes, letter shapes and forms, and letters will support writing. So when you do movement activities, fingerplays, or songs about shapes, you are supporting writing. We provide other example activities later in the chapter that can be used to encourage writing concepts, and we encourage you to alter these activities or develop your own.

Craft Time

Incorporating a short craft time in your storytime is another fun way to incorporate writing concepts. While it is simpler to have craft time prior to or following story-time, some librarians we observed during our study included a craft in the middle of storytime that was based on a book they had just read. Again, this is another place where you can decide what works best for your storytime, space, and community.

Try to include crafts that provide lots of opportunity for fine motor skills, such as drawing, coloring, cutting, and gluing. You can also focus on letters and shapes by having the children make letters from pipe cleaners or yarn; use outlines of letters that children can color or glue sand onto to create sensory letters.

The main point we want you to take away is this: *however you include writing concepts, it should align with your goals as an informal learning environment.* One way to think about writing activities aligning with your storytime goals is to base the activities on the foundational characteristics of play.

- Writing activities in your storytime should be interactive, enjoyable, and active.
- Participation in writing activities should be initiated by the child and supported and scaffolded by you and the caregivers.
- The support and scaffolding of writing activities should be provided through fun and interactive methods.

Most important, throughout all your writing activities, recognize that each child will be at a different skill level, so be sure to emphasize and celebrate every child's effort and the progress that they make.

WHY IS WRITING IMPORTANT?

As the children develop their fine motor skills, they will be able to get their fingers to do what their brain is telling them to do. This helps them to be able to properly hold a pen or pencil. As they practice [those motions] with their fingers and hands, they develop the neural pathways that will allow them to later be able to translate that into what we actually see as writing as opposed to just scribbles.

—**Bonnie Anderson**

You might be wondering why writing is important for storytime. According to the ECRR2 toolkit, writing fits in naturally with reading.[8] Just like reading, writing teaches children that print has meaning, letters represent sounds, and written words represent the oral words they use every day. Given that writing is a key school readiness skill in itself and that it supports other early literacy skills, it should be included as a consistent element of storytimes.[9] In storytime, you can support later writing skills in many different ways. When making gross motor movements in action songs, children must have a sense of themselves in space to be able to position themselves and develop motions for writing. Fingerplays such as "Itsy Bitsy Spider" develop children's fine motor skills and pincer grasp, which are both important precursors to writing. Incorporating writing concepts in storytime also allows you to demonstrate to caregivers that writing and fine motor skills are crucial skills for young children. During writing-related activities, you can also use asides to explain why writing concepts are important.

Writing helps children learn to pay attention to print and connect print to oral language. Thus, children become aware of print concepts, such as the idea that letters make up words and that print progresses from left to right. As children are writing letters, they have to focus on what the letters look like and how they look different from one another, which in turn helps them with alphabetic knowledge.[10] As children are starting to write words they are also developing and solidifying their phonological awareness skills.[11] Finally, working on writing concepts can help children practice narrative skills and demonstrate to children that there are multiple ways to communicate.

Ultimately, incorporating writing concepts in storytime is essential because similar to literacy concepts, children need to be exposed to writing concepts throughout their day and across many environments. Continuous exposure to writing concepts demonstrates to children that writing is an important part of daily life and that it serves multiple purposes and functions.

VPT AND WRITING IN STORYTIMES: HOW DO I DO IT?

In the Project VIEWS2 study, writing concepts were observed in only a small portion of storytimes. Therefore, we feel this is an area that needs emphasis and demonstration, for as we explained above, writing is essential for school readiness and supports early literacy skills. It is understandable that you may be uncertain as how to include writing concepts in your storytime. You may be concerned that your storytime space is not conducive to including writing activities, or that you have too many children at your storytime to include a writing activity. These are all questions that arose during the study.

We want you to realize that you can and should include writing concepts in many ways throughout your storytime. This is not to say you should be providing direct instruction in writing; that is not what storytime is about. However, you can provide opportunities and activities that encourage writing skills. In order to help you understand how this can be done, we have included examples from Bonnie Anderson, children's librarian at Puyallup (Washington) Public Library, for incorporating writing concepts into storytime, based on the three categories from above:

- name recognition and writing
- storytime activities that support writing
- craft time

Then we discuss the types of literacy behaviors present in those activities and how you can extend these into your own storytimes.

Examples of Writing in Storytime

Bonnie incorporates writing concepts throughout her preschool storytimes, starting from the moment the children walk in the door. She encourages the children to make name tags before storytime, includes writing concepts throughout storytime, and does a craft afterward.

BEGINNING OF STORYTIME

Bonnie has a table at the entrance of the storytime space so children and caregivers can stop to make their name tags. She sits at the table and welcomes the children to support their name writing.

> Probably the most specific way that I include name writing is that as the kids enter the storytime area, they make name tags. I don't force them to write their names, but as they see the other kids writing their names, even the youngest ones want to join in. And it may start off as just a little scribble, but then it gets better. Eventually, some of them write so well, I can read their name upside down.
>
> When I started having them write their own name instead of me writing it for them or having parents write it for them, I was amazed at how many kids were motivated to learn the letters of their name and how to write them. I used to just ask the kids their name and I would write it down. And then I started saying, "Okay, can you spell that for me" because that would give them the chance to at least spell the letters. And I realized, Well, if they can spell it, maybe they can write it. So I moved to letting them write their names and sure, sometimes it's a little hard to read, but it was amazing to me how early they actually were able to do it.

VARIATIONS ON NAME WRITING IN STORYTIME

Instead of making name tags each time:
- Have the children write their names on a whiteboard, butcher paper, or a chalkboard.
- Have several pieces of paper laid out on a table where the children can "sign in" or "sign out" of storytime.
- If you offer a craft time, always ask the children to sign their artwork so they get some practice with writing their names.
- If you have a larger crowd at storytime, ask the children to each make a name tag the first time and save the name tags from week to week. Lay out the name tags at the beginning of storytime so the children can find theirs.

By including name writing in storytime, you can encourage many different early literacy skills. Here are some examples of some of the literacy behaviors from the VPT that name writing supports.

Comprehension

In the example above, you can see that the Comprehension domain is supported by questions such as, "What is your name?" and "How do you spell that?" By answering these questions, children demonstrate that they understand the question and are following the conversation.

Print Concepts

You are supporting the Print Concepts domain just through the act of having the children write their names because it helps them to recognize that the print (the letters and words) they are writing conveys a message. You can support print concepts by pointing to the letters as children are writing them on their name tags and asking them to identify the letters. You could also ask them to tell you what their name tag says, which helps to solidify the connection between their names and what they wrote.

Alphabetic Knowledge

While writing their names, children make connections between the letters, their shapes, and their sounds. You can support the Alphabetic Knowledge domain by pointing to the letters as children are writing them on their name tags and asking them to identify the letters. You can also ask them to tell you the sound the letters make.

Writing Concepts

By giving children the opportunity to write their names, you are supporting writing concepts. In addition, you are encouraging them to practice with specific letters that are meaningful to them.

STORYTIME

During storytime, Bonnie uses three fun activities to encourage writing concepts.

1. Letter Puzzles

> We do things like letter puzzles. It's a letter shape and on that shape are pictures of different things that start with that letter and then each of those pictures has been cut off. For example, a letter *H* might have seven pieces, and as I put each piece up on my magnet board, at first they don't realize that I'm putting them together and it's making a shape, but usually by the time the letter is about halfway formed, one of the kids will go, "Ah, that's going to be —" whatever letter it is that we're working with. So I've done that with several letters of the alphabet. Eventually I'll have all of the letters, but right now I think I've got about eight of the letters that I've done and the kids seem to enjoy it. I don't do it every week because then, of course, there would not be the surprise anymore. So, that's a fun one to do.

2. Letter Hunt

> I have a bag full of little stuffed animals and plastic toys and the little magnet letters. I will scatter them on the floor and then sing a little song: "I'm looking for an A, I'm looking for an A, who can find it, who can find it, looking for an A," or whatever letter. And then they all sort through the pile of items to find either the plastic letter or one of the objects that starts with that letter. And, of course, then they'll show me what they found and if they found the letter or an object that starts with the letter, "Great, you found a —" whatever it is. If it isn't quite right, "Oh, that's a —, can you find —"and redirect them to try to find something that does match. Never tell them, "Oh, you messed up," because that would make it not fun anymore.

ADDITIONAL WRITING ACTIVITIES FOR STORYTIMES

For Larger Groups

Writing or painting letters in the air:

- Talk the children through the shape of the letter while modeling how to write it in the air.
- Be sure to talk about the letter, the sound it makes, and some words that start with the letter.
- Have the children draw the letters very big and then very small to incorporate gross and fine motor skills.
- This supports Writing Concepts, Alphabetic Knowledge, and Phonological Awareness domains.

For Baby and Lapsit Storytimes

- Encourage parents to trace letters on their babies' tummies or backs and to talk with their babies about the letters in their names.
- Use props in your songs, like scarves and shakers, that babies can grasp and hold, as this helps to develop their fine motor skills that contribute to later writing skills.
- These support Writing Concepts and Alphabetic Knowledge domains.

For Wiggly Children

One way to get kids up and moving is:

- Put large masking tape letters on the floor of your storytime space and encourage them to walk along the letters.
- While the children are walking the shape of each letter, engage them in a conversation about the letter and the sound it makes.
- Make sure to ask them some words that start with the letter.
- This supports Writing Concepts, Alphabetic Knowledge, and Phonological Awareness as well as gross motor skills.

For Tech Storytimes

Digital tablets can be great tools for supporting writing concepts:

- Draw a letter in a painting app when talking about the shape of the letter.
- Show pictures of letters.
- Show pictures of objects that start with the letter.
- These activities support Writing Concepts, Alphabetic Knowledge, and Phonological Awareness domains.

3. Pointing to Words

Another way I incorporate writing skills is to point to the words in the book as we go along when we are reading the books, especially in some of the books that have words written large; [I] point to the word and wait for the kids to say it, especially if it's repeated. A lot of the kids will figure out the word and repeat it. Then more and more will join in as we go through the book.

Activities such as these can support writing concepts as well as encourage many different early literacy skills in storytime. These activities incorporate many of the literacy behaviors from the VPT.

Alphabetic Knowledge

The letter puzzles activity helps to support alphabetic knowledge by having children focus on the shape of the letter when trying to guess the letter in the puzzle. The letter-hunt activity encourages alphabetic principle by having the children match the letter shape with the letter name. Finally, pointing at individual words in a book helps to support alphabetic knowledge by solidifying the connection between print and verbal words and sounds.

Vocabulary

The letter puzzles can support vocabulary by asking the children to identify the different pictures that make up the letter. With the letter hunt, you can have the children identify the items they find. If possible try to include some items that are not as common to help expose the children to unfamiliar words.

Phonological Awareness

The letter puzzles and letter hunt encourage phonological awareness by reinforcing beginning word sounds when children try to identify the letter puzzle and while looking for items in the pile that start with a certain sound. Pointing at individual words supports phonological awareness by helping to make the connection between the words and letters on the page and the sounds made when spoken aloud.

Writing Concepts

All these activities encourage writing concepts by placing an emphasis on letters, what they look like, and their shapes.

CRAFT TIME

Craft time takes place at the end of Bonnie's storytime.

The craft normally carries through the theme of the books that we've used for the story portion of it. Sometimes it's loosely related, but I find that by doing some sort of a craft that's related to the theme, kids remember it more. At the end when you ask them, "Well, what were the books that we talked about today?" They'll say, "Oh, well we had books about cars today." "Do you remember one of them?" And often they will. Whereas if you don't do a thematic craft, the kids have a harder time because it's not as concrete as when there is something that ties everything together.

We also sometimes turn letters into objects. Of course, turning an S into a snake is the most obvious one, but it might be turning an *H* into a house. We use all sorts of things that they can manipulate with their hands so whether we are painting with Q-tips or paintbrushes or coloring with crayons or felt pens; they have a variety of ways to develop the fine motor skills.

Craft time can support multiple early literacy skills in addition to writing concepts. Literacy behaviors from the VPT can be incorporated in several simple ways.

Communication
Communication skills can be encouraged during craft time by asking children questions about their craft and pausing to give them time to respond. This teaches them to take turns in conversations and helps them learn to pay attention to the speaker.

Language Use
During craft time, if it's related to the book or theme, you can encourage language use by asking questions about the pictures and the story/stories that you read during storytime. You can also prompt the children to tell you stories about their craft or picture.

Writing Concepts
By incorporating a craft time, you are providing time for the children to practice and explore drawing and writing, which reinforces writing concepts.

Bottom Line

When you create activities that encourage writing concepts, you are helping to prepare your storytime children for school and lifelong learning. Keep in mind that the goal is not to turn this into lessons. However you decide to incorporate writing concepts, it should be fun, enjoyable, and developmentally appropriate for your storytime age group. Also, allow for the fact that the children may be at many different levels, so recognize all forms of writing and celebrate the children's efforts.

Don't forget to talk to caregivers about the importance of providing opportunities for children to practice drawing and writing at home, as well as the importance of talking with children about the shapes of letters and how letters are formed.

A WORD FROM THE EXPERT   BONNIE ANDERSON

■ Writing and Interactivity

I incorporate interactivity into the kids' writing by commenting on what they're doing, whether it's a squiggle or it's something really great. But I also use it as a chance for the kids to show off what they have done and tell me the progress they have made, and some of them are really proud when they show me, "Hey, I can write my name now."

Another way to encourage interactivity is to incorporate movement into writing concepts. For example, I hide letters around the storytime room and say, "Okay, everybody look, let's find —" and tell them what we're looking for—"Let's find the W"—and everybody goes racing around the room until they find the letter.

You can also use more of, "Okay, can somebody show me . . ." or, "Here in this book, see this word, what does this first letter sound like?" And some of them will know and some of them won't, but they'll start telling you what it sounds like and then the others will join in. So, you find ways to work with your group.

■ Writing with Different Age Groups

When I do the toddler time as opposed to my preschool storytime, very few of those kids can actually write their names. So, in that case, my first activity of having the kids write their own names doesn't work as well. The parents write the names there, but I can still point out, "Oh, your name is —" whatever it might be. Or I can do "That starts with a —" and point to the letter. And that's probably about as complicated as I get with the toddlers, usually. We don't do a lot of the more advanced spelling, like spelling out the entire word, but I do work on recognizing specific letters. Or we can still [point] to the words as we read so that they're getting the idea that those shapes, those funny squiggles in the book, they mean something. So, if I'm following along with my hand in the book as I'm saying the words, they focus on that and may see: Oh, there's a reason why those squiggles are there and maybe someday they'll mean something to me, too. And rhymes and repetition, of course, that's fun at all ages.

■ How to Share with Parents/Caregivers about Writing

For me, I find that if I just give [caregivers] a very, very brief reason [for incorporating writing skills], maybe once or twice interspersed with the stories and once as we go to the crafts, but no more than that, just keeping it brief and light, so it doesn't feel like I'm telling them they're doing it wrong and it doesn't feel like I'm preaching to them but I'm just giving them some ideas. You know, "Hey, here's something cool you can try"—that seems to work really well.

I also try to give a couple of unobtrusive comments to the parents about why we do crafts and why they should actually let the child do their own cutting or whatever instead of doing it for them. Something like, "We have scissors here, and I know sometimes that that's a scary thing, but that's a great way for kids to develop the fine motor skills that they need to learn to write." Or "You know, these kids may not draw it the way you would draw it, but they have a wonderful chance here to practice using their hands in a different way." Whatever it might be, throw a few unobtrusive comments for the parents. 🖳

WRITING AND SCAFFOLDING

As we have discussed in this chapter, early writing skills are a great fit for storytimes. Knowledge of geometric shapes, letter shapes, and letters, along with fine and gross motor skills, are important early writing skills that you can include in storytime. However, because you may not have previously incorporated these skills, you will want to provide lots of scaffolding at the beginning.

Shapes, Letters, and Names

Letters—in particular, the letters in a child's name—and their shapes are a great way to introduce writing concepts in storytime. Depending on the age and skills of your storytime children, you can start with the basics and then move up to more difficult aspects, again scaffolding the skill for them.

Here is one example of a progression of activities. All these activities can be used with toddlers and preschoolers, and even a couple of the beginning activities can be used with babies. The children may need assistance until they have mastered the skill, so encourage their caregivers to help them.

1. **Start out with an activity that emphasizes the children's names.**

   Sing an opening song like "Hickety, Pickety, Bumblebee" with each child's name. If it is a baby storytime, have the caregivers share each baby's name. (See the sidebar for the words to this song.)

2. **Incorporate a more challenging skill by using an activity that helps the children recognize the first letter of their names.**

   Sing an opening song like "Hickety, Pickety, Bumblebee," but use letters instead of names and have the children jump up if their name starts with that letter.

3. **Move on to an activity in which you talk with children about the other letters in their names.**

   Sing an opening song like "Hickety, Pickety, Bumblebee," but use letters instead of names and have the children jump up if they have that letter anywhere in their name.

4. **Incorporate an activity in which you talk about the shapes of letters.**

   Place a flannel shape on a flannelboard along with two or three letters. Ask the children which letter(s) have that shape. For example, place a circle, then an uppercase *A* and a lowercase *d*.

   Place large flannel letters on a flannelboard and play "Find the Shapes in the Letters." For example, you can find triangles in the letter *A*, a circle in the *O*, and a rectangle in the *H*. Be sure to talk about the letter itself and its overall shape.

HICKETY, PICKETY, BUMBLEBEE

"Hickety, Pickety, Bumblebee" is a great song for including names and letters. Feel free to substitute a variety of actions in order to keep it fun and exciting for the children.

Hickety, pickety, bumblebee, Who can say their name for me?

[Child says name.]

Clap it.
[Everyone claps the syllables in the name while saying it.]

Whisper it.
[Everyone whispers the name.]

5. **Incorporate an activity in which the children trace shapes or letters in the air.**

> With younger children, it may be hard for them to visualize the shape in the air. You can use several pipe cleaners strung together and made into the shape so they can actually see it. Trace it with your finger, then trace it in the air.

> Encourage the children to use other body parts, like a foot or elbow, to make it fun and silly.

6. **Incorporate an activity in which the children notice what is similar and different.**

> Matching games on the flannelboard are a great way to help children notice how objects are similar and different. For example, you might do a mitten match. Each mitten pair has a different color or pattern. You hand out one of a pair to each child and keep the other; each child comes up when you have placed the matching mitten design on the board.

7. **Incorporate an activity in which the children spell their names.**

> Do some name crafts that encourage children to recognize and select the letters in their names. For example, provide precut letters or letter stickers that they can attach to paper.

8. **Finally, include an activity in which the children write their names.**

> Encourage the children to make name tags when they enter storytime. If you do not use name tags, perhaps use a "sign-in" sheet or write on mural paper. They can also sign their crafts at the end of craft time.

Motor Skills

Fine and gross motor skills are crucial for later writing. Since different ages are at different stages of motor skill development, it is important to understand how to scaffold activities for them.

- **With children ages birth to 18 months**. At this age, children are developing some of the beginning muscles needed for later writing by learning to grasp items, pick up items using their index finger and thumb, and learning to take their hands and arms across the midline of their bodies. You can encourage fine and gross motor skills for babies by incorporating songs that have some bigger movements, by including clapping and by using props that they can grasp, like scarves and rattles. Encourage caregivers to help the babies clap and do the hand motions to the songs. Eventually the babies may be able to do the motions on their own.

- **With children ages 18 to 36 months**. At this age, children are further developing their muscles to where they can start to hold a pen or pencil and make some marks and scribbles on a page. Those toward the end of this age range may be able to draw or write some letters or letter-like forms. You can encourage fine motor skills by providing craft time so the children have the opportunity to draw at their own level, from scribbling to more purposeful scribbles where they can tell you what they drew. You can also use fingerplays and activities that use finger motions; just start out with larger hand motions, and once they have mastered those, move to smaller, more detailed hand and finger motions.

- **With children ages 36 to 60 months**. At this age children are moving into drawing pictures and writing some letters—and perhaps their names or other words. You can encourage their fine motor skills by providing craft activities that require more detailed tasks such as gluing, cutting, drawing and coloring. You can also use fingerplays and other activities that use finger motions. Have the younger ones start out with smaller hand motions and then use smaller, more detailed finger motions.

Writing and reading go together; they both represent the spoken word. By understanding and recognizing the skills that young children develop from infancy, we are better able to support later writing through movement activities, sharing books, and building on the preciousness of their own names. Stepping back to take a fresh look at what we already do and ways to build on what we know children enjoy gives us an opportunity to call upon our creativity to supercharge our storytimes.

NOTES

1. Bonnie Anderson has been a children's librarian since 1980, combining several of her greatest passions: kids, reading, learning, acting, and storytelling.

2. Elena Bodrova and Deborah J. Leong, "Play and Early Literacy: A Vygotskian Approach," in *Play and Literacy in Early Childhood: Research from Multiple Perspectives*, ed. Kathy Roskos and James F. Christie (New York: Routledge, 2009), 185–200.

3. Cynthia S. Puranik and Christopher J. Lonigan, "From Scribbles to Scrabble: Preschool Children's Developing Knowledge of Written Language," *Reading and Writing: An Interdisciplinary Journal* 24, no. 5 (2011): 567–89, doi:10.1007/s11145–009–9220–8.

4. Hope K. Gerde, Gary E. Bingham, and Barbara A. Wasik, "Writing in Early Childhood Classrooms: Guidance for Best Practices," *Early Childhood Education Journal* 40, no. 6 (2012): 351–59, doi:10.1007/s10643–012–0531-z.

5. Janet W. Bloodgood, "What's in a Name? Children's Name Writing and Literacy Acquisition," *Reading Research Quarterly* 34, no. 3 (1999): 364, doi:10.1598/RRQ.34.3.5.

6. Puranik and Lonigan, "From Scribbles to Scrabble."

7. Bloodgood, "What's in a Name?", 342–67.

8. Association for Library Services to Children (ALSC) and Public Library Association (PLA), *Every Child Ready to Read, 2nd Edition Kit*, 2011, section 1, 5.

9. Alice Frazeur Cross and Michael Conn-Powers, "A Working Paper: New Information about School Readiness," Early Childhood Center—Indiana University, 2011; Karen E. Diamond, Hope K. Gerde, and Douglas R. Powell, "Development in Early Literacy Skills during the Pre-Kindergarten Year in Head Start: Relations between Growth in Children's Writing and Understanding of Letters," *Early Childhood Research Quarterly* 23, no. 4 (2008): 467–78, doi:10.1016/j.ecresq.2008.05.002.

10. Diamond, Gerde, and Powell, "Development in Early Literacy Skills."

11. Bloodgood, "What's in a Name?", 342–67; Grover J. Whitehurst and Christopher J. Lonigan, "Emergent Literacy: Development from Prereaders to Readers," in *Handbook of Early Literacy Research*, vol. 1, ed. Susan B. Neuman and David K. Dickinson (New York: Guilford Press, 2001), 11–29.

WORKSHEET

Reflection Questions on Writing

1. What is the targeted age group of my storytimes?

   _____

2. What age groups actually attend my storytimes?

   _____

3. How do I model writing to fit the age group(s) of children who attend my storytime using behaviors from the VPT?

   _____

4. How have I been successful in doing so?

   _____

5. How do I model interactivity through writing activities in my storytime?

   _____

6. How have I been successful in doing so?

   _____

7. What activities do I offer that encourage children to write?
   a. What activities am I using that emphasize children's names?
   b. What activities am I using during storytime that emphasize writing concepts, including the development of fine motor skills?
   c. What activities am I using during craft time that encourage writing?

   _____
   _____
   _____
   _____
   _____

8. How do I scaffold writing activities for different ages and abilities in my storytime?

   _____

9. How do I talk with parents/caregivers about writing with their child(ren)?

   _____

10. What would I change for a future storytime to incorporate behaviors around writing interactively in my storytime?

    _____

11. How do I incorporate fun into my writing activities?

    _____

ASSESSING YOUR SUPERCHARGED STORYTIME

I feel like we all want to know that what we're doing has an eventual impact on the growth and development of children, and assessment of our work and evaluating what works—and maybe what's less effective—helps us gauge if that impact will be a positive one.

—Ericka Brunson, Youth Services Librarian, Sylvan Way Branch,
Kitsap (Washington) Regional Library

PROJECT VIEWS2
Exploring Storytime Assessment

THE FIRST PART OF PROJECT VIEWS2, WHAT WE HAVE COVERED UP to now in the book, looked at the impact of the storytime's early literacy content on the children's early literacy behaviors while attending the storytime. As mentioned before, we saw that what storytime providers intentionally do in storytimes *does* influence the behaviors that children exhibit in storytime. In this section, when we talk about storytime assessment, we are not talking about assessing the connection between the storytime provider's and the children's behaviors; we are looking at structures, tools, and methods that allow us in public libraries to improve the impact of our programs.

The Project VIEWS2 researchers focused on public library storytime assessment, for the final years of the grant, and how it relates to the VIEWS2 Planning Tool (VPT). This focus came directly from conversations with practitioners, all of whom were seeing an emergent need to assess and articulate the value of public library storytimes in the lives of people in their communities.

We conducted interviews with thirty-five public library librarians and administrators, asking questions around the following topics:

- types of assessment currently in place, if any;
- perceptions of a need for, and relevance of, assessment to practice;
- benefits and challenges;
- types of tools being used for assessment.

The purpose: to understand as holistically as possible the issue of assessment in public libraries with respect to storytimes.

THE FINDINGS

What these interviews revealed was unsurprising, yet powerful in its pervasiveness: again and again we heard the same hopes and concerns across systems big and small, among both storytime providers and library administrators. Many agree that using assessment to understand the impact of storytimes is valuable both to the practitioner and to the institution as a tool for advocacy. However, many of the challenges that resonated and created issues around development and implementation included a deep concern regarding what is being assessed; how it is being assessed; and the impact of the assessment on the practitioner and practice.

In our study, we found that libraries across Washington State are using many types of assessment to understand the impact and effectiveness of their storytimes. Some of the more common types of assessment that emerged were:

- peer mentoring/coaching (with and without observations of storytime)
- self-reflection practices (spontaneous and intentional)
- administrator observations
- new-hire onboarding/training
- annual reviews
- parent/caregiver assessment

Common benefits and challenges include the following:

- Community building between peers can enable both sharing ideas and improving practice through peer feedback.
- Assessment holds the potential to standardize storytime practice and provide families with evidence-based effective practices (though there were

ASSESSMENT VERSUS EVALUATION

During the interviews we performed as part of the VIEWS2 Exploring Storytime Assessment Study, we have found that the terms *assessment* and *evaluation* are used interchangeably to refer to the same types of processes.

However, we wanted to explore the definitions of the terms so that we could decide which term we should use to describe the practices that are being used with storytime. As a result of this exploration, we developed the definitions of *assessment* as an ongoing process of understanding and revision, and *evaluation*, on the other hand, as a more finite appraisal of the product.

- Assessment is formative and focused on the process.
- Evaluation is summative and focused on the product.

The activities that were described to us during the VIEWS2 Exploring Storytime Assessment Study were, for the most part, formative and focused on developing effective storytime practices to meet the needs of specific communities. Given that most of the activities were centered on professional development and that the library is an informal learning environment, we chose to use the term *assessment* to refer to all the activities that are being used to determine the effectiveness of storytime.

In an assessment, you can also focus on the outcomes you set for your storytime—outcomes that stem from the VPT. For instance, if you decide to focus on vocabulary in your storytime, you can use self-reflection worksheets to help you understand whether the outcome is occurring and how you can improve that outcome for next time. This is an assessment process because you are using the worksheets to continuously improve your storytime planning and delivery.

also concerns about what might be lost in this standardization in terms of individual creativity and imagination).

- Both administrators and librarians want quality storytimes, and they want to include effective practices in their work. But buy-in for assessment is still a challenge because of the possibility that this practice will be tied to performance reviews and potentially damaging.
- Casual peer-to-peer conversation and reflection are also valued, but don't happen enough. Nor are they leveraged as valid forms of assessment; when they do happen, it is often serendipitous.
- Time and staffing are a common concern for everyone: How do we design yet another system that requires an investment of time and staffing? How do we demonstrate its correlation to improved practice and strengthened peer communities?

Assessment on a broad scale can be a way to advocate for the work you do, to articulate your contribution to public value and impact on your community. It can help you to better understand the work you and your peers do for the patrons you serve every day. And for your own growth and development, you can set goals for yourself and use tools that will help you reach those goals. Assessment is a powerful asset in your journey to improve your practice on a continuous basis.

WHAT WE LEARNED FROM THE STUDY

From our interviews, we know that assessment is not a cookie-cutter process and there is no single approach that will work for every library/librarian. On every level—from systems to branches to libraries to librarians—there is a benefit and a challenge to implementing an assessment process and developing an assessment tool. Storytimes are inherently informal, unpredictable events that can differ greatly from week to week. But you can be intentional about including early literacy content, being interactive in how you incorporate that content, and then relying on your community of fellow librarians and storytime providers to support you so that you can improve your own practice. We know that self-reflection and peer mentoring are often spontaneous, informative, and positive processes. In fact, when we provided the training in the VIEWS2 storytime study, we emphasized self-reflection and peer mentoring as ways to focus on and improve practice. The worksheets we offer in the appendix provide a structure by which you can plan and deliver supercharged storytimes while also allowing for individual flexibility, styles, and creativity.

SELF-REFLECTION

~~~~~

Reflection is the process of stepping back from an experience to ponder, carefully and persistently, its meaning to the self.

—M. Daudelin, "Learning from Experience through Reflection," in *Dynamics*

SELF-REFLECTION AND WHY IT IS IMPORTANT

Self-reflection can be an incredibly powerful tool to help you understand if your storytime is achieving the goals that you set. Throughout Project VIEWS2 we saw that storytime providers were reflecting on their storytimes using many different methods and types of tools. We bring up self-reflection here as a method of assessing your own storytimes, measuring against what you have previously done in order to develop and grow your own storytime practices. Self-reflection has been used quite a bit in education to help teachers work on professional development and grow their storytime practices. Teachers, because they often work in isolation (similar to some storytime providers), are encouraged to engage in self-reflection—often by videotaping themselves—to understand and evaluate their own behaviors and actions.[1]

As a storytime provider, you have some flexibility in designing your storytimes to fit the needs of your community, instead of being held to a standard curriculum. Because of this flexibility, you can continually reflect on your storytime content as well as how the children (and parents/caregivers) responded to it in order to understand whether or not your activities were impactful.

One significant benefit to self-reflection is that even if you're in your own library and you're the only one delivering storytime, you can complete an assessment of your storytimes in one form or another, wherever you are. As we will discuss, there are many ways to reflect on your storytime. The most important thing is to find the process and tools that work for you and your storytime and which can also impact and inform your future planning. You may find that reflecting on your storytimes will impact and inform your planning for the next storytime, which will eventually become a cyclical process of planning and reflecting (see figure 7.1).

Figure 7.1

A Picture of Storytime Assessment

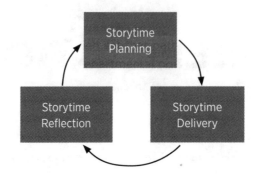

HOW DO I DO IT?

As we have progressed through Project VIEWS2, we have come across many models of self-reflection. All of them hold the benefit of providing you with information and feedback on your own storytime. Because you, your process, your storytimes, your libraries, and your communities are so unique, we understand that what works for one storytime provider may not work for another. As a result, we provide a brief overview of the different models of self-reflection that emerged during the study. We hope that you will try several of these models in order to find what works best for you and your process.

Self-Reflection through the Book

As you worked through this book and completed the worksheets at the end of each chapter, you have actually been engaging in self-reflection of your storytimes. You may have noticed these reflections were specifically targeting the ECRR2 practice that you were working on in that chapter. This was meant to get you thinking about how you are using the important principles of Supercharged Storytimes, such as interactivity and talking to parents.

As you move on to plan your storytimes more broadly using the VPT, keep in mind that you can continue to reflect in a targeted manner to help you assess the success of specific skills and activities that you are emphasizing. We encourage you to keep using the worksheets if they work well for you, but also to realize that you can use a different model of self-reflection for a targeted part of your storytime.

In addition to looking at individual storytime activities and content, it is important to reflect on your storytimes as a whole on a regular basis, too. As such, we have provided worksheets in appendix A for you to use during this longer process.

I think that, for anyone in any job, self-assessment [self-reflection] is key to making improvement and to not getting stuck in a rut. It is important for anybody who's doing any kind of educational work to constantly be learning. Self-assessment is a continual process that is valuable, and I don't think it's just something that's only pertinent to storytimes but to all the things we do.

—VIEWS2 participant

- The short-term worksheet can be used more regularly throughout your storytime series to facilitate regular self-reflection. This worksheet also includes a section for planning to help you work toward the cyclical process of having your planning and reflecting informing each other; ultimately helping you to think about what you have done in the past storytime and what you might want to change or alter for future storytimes.
- The long-term reflection worksheet can be used occasionally—mainly when you are finishing a storytime series or when you have refocused the goals of your storytime and want to reflect on the progress.

The whole purpose of self-reflection is to help you grow and develop effective practices. Feel free to alter or build on these worksheets to suit your needs. If the worksheets have not been useful for you, we encourage you to try other models that we detail below.

Self-Reflection in the VIEWS2 Storytime Study

We intentionally incorporated self-reflection as a piece of the training that took place during the VIEWS2 Storytime Study because we wanted to emphasize the importance of self-reflection in developing effective practices. During that training, we asked the storytime providers to reflect on their storytimes by:

- making note of behaviors they had chosen from the VPT;
- thinking about the activities they had used to incorporate those behaviors; and
- thinking about how the children responded to the activities and behaviors.

By taking time to reflect on how the children responded, the storytime providers were able to assess whether to revise the activity or keep it as is. The storytime providers were then able to share information from their reflection with their peers in the webinars, which allowed them to get feedback and advice on their activities and how to revise them. Because the storytime providers were using the VPT as part of their storytime planning, we included the VPT as part of their reflection to help link their reflection to the next iteration of their planning.

Another method for self-reflection that organically emerged after the VIEWS2 training was the use of a video camera by a storytime provider to record his or her own storytime. During the VIEWS2 Storytime Study we videorecorded the storytime providers while they were offering their program. Because of this, some of the providers began to record their own storytimes so they could watch themselves. They were able to refer back to the video instead of just relying on memory, and they could see things that they normally would not be aware of or be able to view. They essentially were able to gain a "third-party" perspective on the delivery of their own storytime activities. As one VIEWS2 Librarian told us, "I have learned a great deal from recording my own storytimes. With some of them I thought, "I didn't know I did that." But for the most part, I really enjoyed watching the videos that I made, and I'm seeing things that I do during storytime: facial expressions or reactions, body language, and [other] different things, too. I'm really learning a lot from this practice."

VIDEOING CONSIDERATIONS

Here are some things to consider when thinking about recording your storytime:

- Check with your library system about any needed permissions to video storytime participants. Though you may intend only to be recording yourself, you inevitably will get some children in the video recording.

- Talk to your storytime participants a few weeks in advance of recording so they are aware of when you are recording, why you are recording, and what you are going to do with the recording.

- Figure out in advance where to place the camera in order to get the best view of your storytime program delivery (especially if you move around).

- Find a place where families can sit and be completely out of camera range if they do not want to be included in the recording.

- Finally, find a staff member or volunteer to sit by your camera and tripod when recording because, as we have discovered from experience, little children love video cameras!

Do you have a video camera or a cell phone with video capability? Then we encourage you to try recording one of your storytimes. We think you will find that you will learn a lot from the process. If you do decide to record your own storytime, please see the sidebar for some things to consider before you begin. Recording your storytimes can be a bit time consuming, so it may be something that you only want to do a few times a year. However, the time spent is worth it because it will provide you with great insight into the storytimes that you deliver. This is also a nice way to receive "feedback" especially if you are in a small library, far from your peers. And it doesn't have to be high-tech!

Self-Reflection in the VIEWS2 Exploring Storytime Assessment Study

One of the biggest challenges that we found in our assessment research was that many storytime providers do not have much time to reflect, so they use quick, spontaneous methods of self-reflection. However, we did talk to other providers who felt self-reflection was an important part of their storytime planning process, so they were more intentional with the process, completing it either after a storytime or while planning for the next one.

The spontaneous, quick model that many storytime providers are using involves mentally comparing their storytimes and practices against other early literacy and storytime tools and resources they encounter in their daily responsibilities. The tools and resources they are using are ones you can use too, such as storytime books (including *Step Into Storytime*, by Saroj Ghoting and Kathy Klatt,[2] or *Storytimes for Everyone*, by Saroj Ghoting and Pamela Martin-Diaz[3]), storytime blogs, ECRR, a library system's storytime guidelines or checklist, and the VPT. Providers are using these tools mainly to determine whether they are actually including the content and skills that they intend to include. While this model is a great way to double check your practices, we want to encourage you to go one step further and be more intentional and purposeful with your own self-reflection.

More intentional models of self-reflection varied quite a bit across storytimes providers. Most providers did place an emphasis on being aware of the children's actions and behaviors to help assess the success and impact of the books and activities that were included. Some providers wrote down those observations of the children's behaviors after each storytime, along with elements (books, songs, activities, etc.) of the storytime to allow them to reflect on and track the impact of those elements. Other storytime providers used intentional self-reflection on a less frequent basis. Some videotaped and then watched their storytimes (as we discussed above). Others blogged or kept a journal about their storytime practices, which allowed them time to reflect on and write about the impact and success of their storytime practices. Finally, in the process of writing monthly or quarterly reports, some storytime providers had the opportunity to reflect on their storytimes. "We have to do a monthly report for our branches and for the youth services department," says one VIEWS2 participant, "so that's the time to reflect on our programming and what we thought went well; areas for improvement; anything that we might have noticed that worked; and things that we were just not doing again."

As you can see, intentional self-reflection can be more time consuming. However, it does not have to be done every week. Find a schedule and model that works for you. We hope that you will find self-reflection to be a useful tool that helps you grow and develop effective storytime practices that truly meet the needs of your storytime community.

Self-Reflection Using the VPT

The VPT itself can be a powerful reflection tool. Because it provides children's behaviors under each early literacy domain and explains how those behaviors correspond to the behaviors that you are incorporating into storytime, the VPT makes it easy for you to see whether your early literacy activities are having the impact on the children's early literacy skills that you intend. In fact, observing children's behaviors during the storytime is a key part of self-reflection. It gives us the opportunity to note if they are engaged as well as to note how they are reacting to the early literacy behaviors we are intentionally emphasizing. Keep in mind that while the VPT gives examples of what the provider can do and what behaviors are reflected in the children—it is not all encompassing.

In order to understand the impact of the activities you plan around VPT behaviors, choose a domain of the VPT and take a look at the children's behaviors that are listed to the right of the behaviors that you chose. You should start to see those behaviors in your storytime children as you utilize the activity over multiple weeks. Keep in mind that children need time to learn and adjust to the activities and skills, so you may not see early literacy behaviors right away. In addition, you can also use the VPT in reverse: refer to the children's section for the types of early literacy skills your storytime children are already demonstrating. Having that understanding will help you to target which early literacy skills the children aren't demonstrating, with which they might need more support. This is another example of how information from your reflection helps inform your storytime planning, making your storytimes more impactful and tailored toward your community.

> Effective practitioners take time to step back and carefully observe the behaviors of their children and take time to reflect upon their own behaviors and the purposes of their actions.
>
> — Colette Gray and Sean MacBlain, *Learning Theories in Childhood*

WHAT HAVE WE LEARNED?

Now that you are aware of the multiple models for self-reflection that we encountered in the study, we wanted to share some of the things that we have learned about storytimes and the self-reflection process:

- Intentionality is crucial—our research demonstrates that being intentional about including early literacy makes a difference in children's early literacy outcomes. Your intentional focus can be supported through ongoing self-reflection.
- The children's behaviors are a vital source of feedback to help you understand the impact of your storytime.
- The VPT can serve as a powerful tool to support your self-reflective process and understand that you are making a difference through what you do.

- There is not a universal process that will fit all libraries and all storytime providers.

Given this, we hope that you find a model that works well for you, your needs, and your process. We encourage you to be intentional about self-reflection of your storytimes and carve out time to engage in it on a regular basis. Taking particular note of the children's reactions and early literacy behaviors in storytime, in conjunction with the VPT during the self-reflective process, will provide you with outcomes to understand the impact of your storytimes.

NOTES

1. Matt Collette, "Bringing Fred Rogers Forward" *School Library Journal*, July 23, 2015, www.slj.com/2015/07/standards/early-learning/bringing-fred-rogers-forward/.
2. Saroj Nadkarni Ghoting and Kathy Fling Klatt, *STEP into Storytime : Using StoryTime Effective Practice to Strengthen the Development of Newborns to Five-Year-Olds* (Chicago: ALA Editions, 2014).
3. Saroj Nadkarni Ghoting and Pamela Martin-Díaz *Storytimes for Everyone! Developing Young Children's Language and Literacy* (Chicago: ALA Editions, 2013).

PEER MENTORING IN THE FIELD

~~~~~~

Observation and assessment are the essential tools of watching and learning with which practitioners can both establish the progress that has already taken place and explore the future.

—Cathy Nutbrown, "Watching and Learning: The Tools of Assessment,"
in Teaching Assistants: Curriculum in Context

PEER MENTORING AND WHY IT IS IMPORTANT

Peer mentoring, also called peer coaching, is a collaborative way to approach storytime assessment. We emphasize it here because throughout Project VIEWS2 we saw evidence of the importance of peer connections and peer feedback in storytime planning and delivery. Sharing ideas, talking through what worked and what needs practice, encouraging one another—these are all ways for you to improve and grow in your work, buoyed by the energy and expertise of your community of colleagues. We encourage you to try to implement a kind of peer mentoring process.

Here are some thoughts from providers we interviewed in our Exploring Storytime Assessment Study that highlight the benefits they see in using peer mentoring in their work:

> I always try to evaluate how any given storytime has gone. I've been doing it for a lot of years, so most of them go well, but every once in a while, there's something that didn't work as well as I had planned and I try to figure out why. And I'm lucky to have another children's librarian at my library to compare notes.

■ ■ ■

It's very important to include some kind of assessment component to everything that we're doing. Otherwise, we're not learning how to do things more effectively. Furthermore, by training all storytime presenters on how to coach each other in a non-threatening, supportive way, it set the stage for presenters to focus attention on what's working and what's not, to create and share effective practices in delivery of their programs, and to encourage, nudge and mentor parents to do more at home. It ups the ante in "team learning." We want to be sure that our children services are constantly improving. And that the impact we're having on the families and the kids are such that they're ready for school, eager to learn, and inspired to keep coming back to the library.

—Dorothy Stoltz, Programming & Outreach Services Manager, Carroll County (Maryland) Public Library

It's helpful to see your storytime from someone else's eyes because it's easy to get stuck doing the same thing over and over again, or to not realize what an impact you actually do have on people. So it's really nice to hear from someone else how it's actually happening.

▪ ▪ ▪

It's reassuring that other people are dealing with the same stuff, [that] they hear your problems. I almost feel like it's a team-building thing.

▪ ▪ ▪

For this book, we interviewed three individuals (two administrators and one story-time provider) from three systems (Carroll County in Maryland, and Pierce County and Kitsap Regional, both in Washington) to learn more about the peer mentoring processes they have in place and what successes and challenges they face. Our goal is to provide you with an in-depth look at three examples of peer mentoring. Keep in mind as you read this section that each library and community is unique; take from these case studies what you think fits with your environment. It is unlikely that there is a one-size-fits-all approach to assessing a program that is as personal, creative, and wonderfully informal as storytime!

CASE STUDY 1

Creating a Learning Culture

Lead Contact: Dorothy Stoltz, Programming & Outreach Services Manager, Carroll County (Maryland) Public Library
Carroll County is a rural/suburban community located forty-five minutes northwest of Baltimore, with a population of approximately 167,000. Although Carroll County is considered a middle-class community, there are significant pockets of poverty. Carroll County Public Library (CCPL) has six full-service branches and three mobile service vehicles.

> Our learning philosophy is to create "a learning culture that inspires employees to achieve excellence leading to a passion for internal and external customer service. The role of all library staff in this culture is to embody innovation, creativity, learning, and risk taking in an atmosphere of respect, support, and trust."
>
> —Dorothy Stoltz

The Assessment Model
CCPL developed their formal assessment process from a desire to create a culture of innovation and community service among their staff. The process itself is surprisingly simple and in fact benefits both parties. Storytime providers are encouraged to develop peer relationships that serve as mentorships. Sometimes these relationships are geographically co-located; at other times they are farther afield.

During the storytime planning process, Storytime Provider A uses an observation form with general assessment questions to help her decide on a focus for her storytime. Let's say she decides to emphasize fingerplays, knowing their importance as an early learning activity. Then her peer observer, Storytime Provider B, observes and notes how A incorporates fingerplays into her storytime, using the same form. After the program is over, A and B give each other some time to sit and reflect on what's just taken place. This enables each individual to focus and center on the topic to be discussed. Then A and B engage in a constructive discussion around fingerplays in storytime—specifically, what went well and what could be strengthened for next time.

One particularly powerful aspect to this process is the fact that it benefits both providers. It is natural that as B is observing A, B is reflecting on his own practice and what he might be able to emphasize and incorporate to improve how he uses fingerplays and engages early literacy behaviors in his storytimes. "The discussion becomes reciprocal, where they are learning from each other, with the coach reflecting on their own practice while providing feedback on what they just observed," Stoltz points out. "The coach might include things like how they might do something or what they find successful as well as what they liked in the storytime they observed."

This mentoring-through-observation process occurs both at the peer and supervisor level, with experienced and new staff alike, though to varying degrees and with different forms. There is a long-observation form that is used by new staff initially, and a short-observation form used with all staff. These observations typically take place twice a year.

Peer feedback can also take place at an informal level, too, and Carroll County is no exception. After storytime, after a parent workshop, during the cleanup process, storytime providers engage in discussions about what worked, what could be improved upon; and they share ideas for next time. This informal process can be seen as part of building and refining those peer relationships that then enables supportive feedback to improve practice. These conversations—though they are impromptu and quick—also foster a culture that values learning, development, and innovation.

Emphasizing an Early Literacy Partnership

Lead Contact: Judy Nelson, Customer Experience Manager—Youth, Pierce County (Washington) Library System

Pierce County Library System serves a population of more than 500,000 people in Pierce County, Washington, encompassing nineteen locations and various outreach services over 1,800 square miles. It contains "very diverse socioeconomic communities that range from very wealthy to rural areas," Judy says. "All of these different communities participate in the library, but their needs are going to be very different and their expectations are very different. And I need my librarians to be talking to me and to each other about what they see their needs are currently. Because no two communities are exactly alike."

The Assessment Model

Pierce County's model grew from Carroll County's model, with adaptations to fit a different library system and community. This assessment process has three parts:

1. Peer-to-peer sharing among youth services staff based on peer observations of storytimes.
2. Training site supervisors to know what they're observing when they visit a storytime.
3. Continuous dialogue and advocacy around the importance of early learning as a focus for libraries among all levels of library staff.

The peer-to-peer sharing begins with a storytime observation, after which the observing peer completes a worksheet structured around the five ECRR practices. The observer is encouraged to include information such as overall observations, what stood out for each practice, and what they had not seen before. The form ends with a space for "the one idea that I would like to steal," which gives the observer a chance to reflect on their own practices as well as what they observed.

The youth service librarians are asked to share these observations at youth service meetings to facilitate further discussion; they also post the completed worksheets on a shared drive in the library system. The observations take place twice a year, as do the youth service meetings. The emphasis is on sharing feedback in a neutral, nonthreatening way, using a playful, positive framework. This is perhaps the most informed aspect of the whole assessment process, as these peers are trained in Every Child Ready to Read (ECRR), and some of them participated in the recent Supercharged Storytimes program presented by OCLC. "Being able to execute the practices is one half of the equation," Judy says, "being able to spot what incorporating the practice looks like is the other." Many of these storytime providers understand early literacy skills and know how to plan and deliver supercharged storytimes, creating a strong mentorship environment. This process enables connections and information sharing across geographical distances in this large library system.

The administrative process involves a training and modeling of storytimes for site supervisors of youth service librarians and storytellers, using manager training observation sheets developed from ECRR2 and then further customized. This process helps supervisors better understand what they should be looking for and seeing in a storytime and thus provide meaningful feedback at the visits and in performance reviews. In many cases, managers do not have youth service backgrounds, which can potentially lead to issues of trust and buy-in for both parties when administrators are providing feedback on programs with which they do not have any experience. Through the training, both parties can feel informed and equipped to assess and discuss the program and the outcomes in a positive way. These administrative trainings take place annually.

Lastly, ongoing advocacy both within the library and throughout the community is key. Strong peer mentoring relationships thrive in an atmosphere that values the practice of storytimes and the importance of early learning. Judy mentions that the Pierce County community has developed an expectation of early learning in the services that the public library provides, and she counts this as a success: "the community expects us to provide this and asks, how are you going to do this? And that's invaluable. You can't buy that advertising, so to speak."

The process at Pierce County grew from the Carroll County process, adapted in three main ways:

- Considering the different-size library system and the relative distance between branches and peer librarians
- Including managers in the process, expecting them to include assessment in their annual performance reviews
- Bringing in community needs as part of the assessment process

Once again, it is important to look at what others do in terms of what would fit in your own system and community.

Building a Mentoring Community across Distances

Lead Contact: Ericka Brunson, Youth Services Librarian,
Sylvan Way Library, Kitsap (Washington) Regional Library

Kitsap Regional Library serves a population of 250,000 people in Kitsap County, Washington, encompassing nine libraries and various outreach services.

This case study is a particularly interesting one because it features a librarian who was part of the VIEWS2 study. Ericka has a unique perspective in terms of experiencing the research training firsthand as well as the data collection, giving her and her colleagues the idea to develop their process of assessment. This case study also features a collaborative process with providers and an administrator.

In many ways the process at Kitsap shares many common elements with the processes at Carroll and Pierce: peer-to-peer interactions, observations, and discussion in regular meetings. However, Ericka and her colleague Greta Bergquist decided to use video cameras to begin the conversations with their peers about how to supercharge their storytimes based on the Project VIEWS2 research. They asked a colleague to record storytimes provided by librarians in their system. Next, the youth services manager, Shannon Peterson, assigned videos for the librarians to watch and then discuss at a monthly meeting. The librarians talked about what they observed in terms of which early literacy behaviors were present in the programs.

For the first round of observations, the librarians focused on alphabetic knowledge and phonological awareness (which support the decoding aspect of later reading) in order to keep the scope of the early literacy observations manageable for each video discussion. In addition, they had the same person film all the storytimes. They knew that the process would take time and require lots of buy-in from participants, so they are now focusing primarily on what is working well and what can be observed in the videos. Constructive criticism will come later as the positive, collaborative atmosphere continues to be built and strengthened. "We're just looking in different places in each video for something they've done that's really great, that will spark discussion and dialogue about what we're doing in our individual storytimes," Ericka says. "And then we also look for places where we can provide some suggestions for improvement. It's a very, very laid-back peer assessment."

The video sharing process has two steps:

1. Two videos are uploaded at a time to a shared drive, and all the librarians view the videos individually in preparation for the next monthly meeting.
2. At the meeting, the librarians discuss the videos and what they noticed during the observations. "I think because we don't have the time and opportunity to really go view other people's storytimes, it worked really well with how our meetings are structured," Ericka says. "We know that once a month we're all going to be together and have that time to discuss things. So this was a great way to just start an assessment process and be able to have it work with our own schedules."

THE GOOD, THE TOUGH, AND THE LESSONS IN BETWEEN

There are many broad benefits and challenges across these various case studies. Implementing an assessment process has led to a greater understanding across each system about the importance of early literacy and children's services for the community. However, assessment requires buy-in and trust, as well as time and resources.

Dorothy at Carroll County emphasized how this assessment process elevated the quality of storytimes since its implementation in 2007: it has "institutionalized that we are paying attention to how to be extremely effective even if we're not using the peer coaching to its maximum benefits." On the other hand, the system faced some ongoing staff turnover that presented a challenge to the peer mentoring process because it changed the organizational structure and impacted existing peer relationships. In addition, providers struggle with the question "How do you continue to make peer coaching a priority while trying to balance other programs and services?"

Judy Nelson at Pierce County also mentioned particular challenges, such as being part of a union environment and adhering to contract language; bringing managers up to a level where they feel they're qualified to observe and assess; connecting assessment to advocacy; and focusing on maintenance and sustainability: "As we look at new budgeting and new initiatives and stuff, where does early learning fit into that in the whole storytime component?" But for Judy, the successes are equally as important. "We have taken the time to infuse all the levels of staff with the understanding that anything around early learning is important," she says. "We are trying to make sure that everybody has that kind of customer focus regardless of what the age of the person is and that just takes time. And in any kind of learned behavior, it takes a little time and you have to pay attention to it and you have to reward it. The community expects us to provide quality early learning programs and services, and PCLS must always evaluate how we are going to do this."

Ericka Brunson at Kitsap highlighted the fact that their assessment process encourages discussion and excites everyone about early learning, early literacy, and why they're doing what they're doing: "Everyone's really stepped forward and come on board, and it was just important that we had a shared understanding of why we were doing what we're doing. We can use this process as a stepping-stone for us to get to that shared vision and the impact that we want to make." Idea sharing is also a big benefit coming out of assessment for her system, she says. "People are getting so many great suggestions and so much positive feedback that it's helping them in how they develop their story times and helping them think about some of the stuff that they're doing."

Time investment is an issue, though, Ericka points out. "The slow pace in getting [the assessment process] started and forming official ways to assess our programs could be a challenge, but again, it's important to our system that what we're doing aligns with our goals and visions." Buy-in, too, can be a challenge: "At first I think people were a little apprehensive about filming themselves and about being evaluated in that environment."

SO WHAT HAVE WE LEARNED?

We have learned that librarians are sharing informally on a regular basis, asking each other for ideas and feedback in the hopes of improving their own practice. We know that building a community of trusted colleagues helps facilitate and sustain a peer mentoring or coaching assessment process that gives storytime providers constructive guidance and support. And a more formal process of assessment requires a deep knowledge of the library system, staff, and the community they serve in order to best understand the practice of storytime.

So what does our model of peer mentoring look like, based on what we learned in our study and in these interviews?

1. Storytime providers can plan their storytimes using feedback and ideas from their peers.
2. They can partner with a colleague to observe how each person delivers storytimes, providing feedback that helps to identify how goals have been met and how new goals can be set.
3. They can deepen their reflection process to then inform their planning for the next storytime through peer feedback and insight.

Assessment doesn't have to be a scary event—it can be positive and rewarding. It can help you continue to serve your ever-changing community in the best ways.

THE BIG PICTURE
Incorporating Assessment in Your Storytime Practice

The specific information gathered from [outcome-based evaluation] changes the focus of what is generally good for children to what a specific library can do to meet the needs of the actual children who will use the library.

—**Eliza T. Dresang, Melissa Gross, and Leslie Holt,**
Dynamic Youth Services through Outcome-Based Planning and Evaluation

HOW DOES EVERYTHING FIT TOGETHER?

At this point you have read about self-reflection and peer mentoring as two types of storytime assessment to help you develop more effective practices and better tailor your storytimes to meet the needs of your community. In this chapter, we look at how self-reflection and peer mentoring can be used to provide information on the outcomes of your storytimes. Outcome-based processes are powerful ways to gain information that you can use to advocate for your storytimes and other programs, and to further develop your own practices.

Keep in mind that we decided to use the term *assessment* to describe the processes that were occurring with storytime, like self-reflection or peer mentoring, because we defined assessment as being ongoing and focused on revision. However, when we start to talk about outcome-based processes, the lines between assessment and evaluation begin to blur. An outcome-based process is really more evaluative—because it focuses on the product or the outcomes. However, it can fit seamlessly into your assessment process, which is more formative and focused on the process of developing more effective storytimes.

SO WHAT ARE STORYTIME OUTCOMES?

What do we mean when we say "outcomes"? You might think we're talking about counting how many people attended the storytime or how many books were checked out afterward. And those can be outcomes, depending on what you're hoping to learn. But in this book, outcomes represent the difference that your storytime is making in the children's early literacy behaviors. When you look at the VPT, you see behaviors that you, the storytime provider, can offer. The corresponding children's behaviors are the outcomes that you are looking for in the children who are attending your storytimes.

Just as a reminder, as we use the terms:

- Assessment is a formative process. It is ongoing and focused on revision.
- Evaluation is a summative appraisal and is focused on the end product.

The outcome information that you get from an outcome-based process can be used for advocacy as well as for helping you understand where your storytime is effective and where it could use some strengthening. As a result it can feed right back into your planning process helping you to supercharge your storytime. This shows us that with storytime, assessment and evaluation can happen together.

An outcome-based model that fits well with supercharged storytimes is the Outcome-Based Planning and Evaluation (OBPE) model, as developed for youth services by Dresang, Gross, and Holt.[1] The model, fully described in *Dynamic Youth Services through Outcome-Based Planning and Evaluation*, was developed as a result of Project CATE (Children's Access to [and use of] Technology Evaluation), which examined children's use of technology in public library settings. The CATE OBPE model provides a framework for children's and youth library staff to incorporate outcomes in the planning and assessment of their programs. In the CATE OBPE model, "the planning and evaluation are inseparable, with the planning process incorporating the iterative evaluation. Planning is not finished at any one point in time but rather is ongoing and continually influenced and modified by the frequent evaluation activities."[2] Keep in mind that even though this quote uses the term *evaluation*, it is still talking about what we are calling *assessment*. Figure 9.1, from *Dynamic Youth Services through Outcome-Based Planning and Evaluation*, lays out the OBPE framework.

> ◗ A supercharged storytime is one that demonstrates early literacy behaviors and one whose outcomes are based on those behaviors so that providers can understand the impact of the storytime.

Figure 9.1

CATE Outcome-Based Planning and Evaluation Model

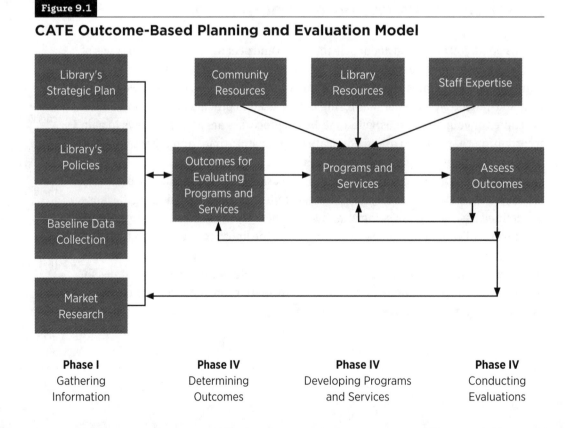

Phase I	Phase IV	Phase IV	Phase IV
Gathering Information	Determining Outcomes	Developing Programs and Services	Conducting Evaluations

This model represents an outcome-based planning and assessment process that you can apply to your storytime planning. We will walk you through the main points of this framework and explain where self-reflection, peer mentoring, planning, and the VPT fit into this model. This way you will understand the big picture and know how to put everything together. See *Dynamic Youth Services through Outcome-Based Planning and Evaluation* if you want to know more.

Planning an Outcome-Based Supercharged Storytime

In the OBPE framework above, you can see that there are various pieces that inform the outcome-based planning process. Many of these will look familiar to you and may be things you consider and turn to for information in your planning process. We're going to focus on the middle three boxes and the process they represent.

First, you see *outcomes for evaluating programs and services.* The domains and behaviors in the VPT can serve as these outcomes for early literacy. Throughout this book, as you have been supercharging your storytime, you have also been planning to use outcomes in order to deliver an outcome-based storytime, which in the framework above is the *programs and services.*

You can plan your supercharged or outcome-based storytime however you feel comfortable with the VPT. You can broadly decide you would like to focus on one of the domains, such as Vocabulary, as your early literacy outcome. As such, you would include vocabulary behaviors in your planning. Or you can be more specific and choose certain behaviors as early literacy outcomes and work on incorporating those in your planning. This is your outcome-based planning process.

When planning with early literacy outcomes, the most important piece is the intentionality. Be aware of:

- which early literacy outcomes you are incorporating;
- how you are incorporating them; and
- how you are articulating them to the parents/caregivers at some point(s) during the storytime.

This way, you can refer back to the outcomes when you begin to assess or evaluate your storytimes.

In the framework above, the *programs and services* stage is where your community of peers can play a role. When you deliver a storytime and invite a colleague to observe and provide feedback, you're relying on and building on staff expertise for that outcome-based program. This is one way that peer mentoring is represented in this model.

Assessing an Outcome-Based Supercharged Storytime

You will see that the next stage in the OBPE framework is to *assess outcomes.* There are many forms of assessment that you can use at this stage in the framework. For the purposes of this book, we emphasize self-reflection and peer mentoring as the types of assessment in this stage because they are the best suited to provide you with information and feedback necessary to grow and develop your storytime practice.

Previously, we touched on examining the children's early literacy behaviors or outcomes during self-reflection. We want to reiterate that you can assess the children's early literacy outcomes during self-reflection as well as the peer mentoring processes. Once you have identified your VPT domains and behaviors during your planning process, you are ready to assess the corresponding early literacy outcomes. To do this, be aware of the children's behaviors during your storytime. You can do this in a few different ways.

1. If you are alone, you can take mental notes of the children's behaviors, when possible, during storytime.
2. You can also record the children (please see our video recording sidebar in chapter 7 for things to consider) so you can observe their behavior after storytime.
3. If a peer storytime provider or staff member is available, they could observe and take notes about the children's behaviors during your storytime.
4. Following storytime, you could ask the caregivers about the children's behaviors.

Regardless of which method you use, once you have information about the children's early literacy behaviors, you can use that information in your self-reflection and peer mentoring processes to understand if your storytime achieved the early literacy outcomes you intended to emphasize. By comparing the behaviors to the children's behaviors listed in the VPT, you can see how they align to the outcomes that you identified.

For example, if you were focusing on vocabulary outcomes, you would compare the children's behaviors to the behaviors in the Vocabulary domain. In addition, you can also go broader and examine the children's behaviors in relation to all VPT behaviors—not just the outcomes that you chose to emphasize—to gain an understanding of the comprehensive set of early literacy outcomes that your storytime is supporting. Seeing how your storytime supports a variety of early literacy outcomes enables you to advocate for the impact of your storytime with your community, as well as continue to deepen your self-reflection planning and assessment process.

WHAT DOES THIS MEAN FOR YOUR PROCESS?

You are now aware of some different models of self-reflection and peer mentoring, and you have an understanding of how to incorporate early literacy outcomes into these processes. You are almost ready to plan your own process.

The final item that we want to cover is how self-reflection and peer mentoring fit together and why you may want to use both processes in your overall assessment program. Let's discuss frequency of assessment. Self-reflection depends only on your own schedule, so you can do it as often as you like. As a result, it is the most likely type of assessment you'll perform on a regular, ongoing basis. Peer mentoring requires having someone to observe your storytimes, so it can take a bit more time and effort. It may be easier to conduct these peer observations on a biannual

Figure 9.2

Self-Reflection and Peer Mentoring Working Together

or quarterly basis. Thus, your assessment program can include self-reflection on a regular basis and peer mentoring on an occasional basis. In addition, self-reflection fits quite naturally into peer mentoring, as seen in the Carroll County and Kitsap County processes—when you participate in the peer mentoring process, you are also engaging in reflection on your own practice.

Given that self-reflection and peer mentoring naturally fit together, we encourage you to include both in your assessment program because both can benefit your own professional development. (See fig. 9.2.). Self-reflection is important because you are the one that is most familiar with your storytime and the children who attend. Therefore you are most qualified to interpret the behaviors of the children and understand what worked well and what did not. Also, self-reflection will provide you with the most consistent and convenient feedback on your storytime practices. Peer mentoring is valuable to your practice because, from time to time, you need an unbiased, outside view of your practice from someone who is generally familiar and experienced with storytime practices. Together, both types of assessment provide you with the most comprehensive feedback and evaluation of your practice. We cannot emphasize enough how planning and delivery feed into each other and can be strengthened and improved by self-reflection and peer mentoring.

Now that we've presented CATE OBPE, an overall framework for evaluating storytime, and discussed two different approaches—self-reflection and peer mentoring—for assessing public library storytimes, we encourage you to think about how you want to develop your own process for assessing your storytimes. In order to support you, our experts have shared some tips for you to consider when implementing self-reflection and peer mentoring in your own library.

FINAL WORDS FROM THE STORYTIME ASSESSMENT EXPERTS
ERICKA BRUNSON, JUDY NELSON, AND DOROTHY STOLTZ

Clear intention: Be really, really clear about why you're doing assessment. Understand that it can't just be about making sure the librarians do it right. If that's your only reason for doing it, then that's a punitive reason and you've missed the "we're trying to do this to improve ourselves" aspect of it.

—JUDY NELSON

Outcomes: It's important that you know why you're developing a way to assess your work. So have a clear outcome in mind and then set that path to get there. Our outcomes are informed by our system goals and our departmental goals but we are constantly looking at what we're doing and assessing the impact that we have on the community and trying to find ways to continuously make it better.

—ERICKA BRUNSON

Peer network: Make sure you really embed the idea that early learning and learning from each other is critical, that nobody's going to be the complete expert, and the best way to be better is for everyone to constantly share knowledge. I think using the peer-to-peer model is less threatening in many cases as long as you help all the staff do it in a positive way. Build a strong peer-to-peer communication piece.

—JUDY NELSON

Time: Nothing has to be perfected overnight. It's important to allow room for success and failure, trial and error, and discovering what's right for your library, for you, and for the community that you're serving.

—ERICKA BRUNSON

Staff support: Get administration on board. And at the same time, find a couple of people who really get it and appreciate it in your frontline staff so that you have motivating energy.

—DOROTHY STOLTZ

Organizational support: Find ways to institutionalize it so that it doesn't go to the wayside. When a library creates a learning philosophy, where each employee is responsible for their own learning, it can connect staff to the library's purpose to support human growth. A library's self-discipline to grow and learn as an organization in order to serve its community magnifies the possibilities and the opportunities to be able to do so.

—DOROTHY STOLTZ

These recommendations emphasize the importance of planning and evaluating storytime programs with broad library system outcomes in mind. Aligning with these outcomes can contribute to coordinated advocacy by providing a clear sense of purpose that unites programming and services under common themes.

Our initial recommendation is that libraries design and implement a planning and assessment process that is centered around outcomes of program impact on children, families, and community; modeling appropriate practices; continuously improving practice; and working with families to get their children ready for school. The peer mentoring aspect of this process can cultivate a culture of trust and collaboration, enabling storytime providers to innovate in a safe environment. The reflective nature of this process facilitates a positive and informed conversation between provider and supervisor, focused on celebrating and improving current practice to continue to serve the community in the best way possible.

How can you help bring this recommendation to your library?

TALKING TO YOUR ADMINISTRATOR ABOUT SUPERCHARGED STORYTIMES

We encourage you to meet and talk regularly with your administrator(s) to facilitate open communication about your programs and your goals for your programs. Share anecdotes from parents, caregivers, and kids that showcase the great work you're doing and the connections you're building in your community. Discuss how you are using assessment, including self-reflection and peer mentoring, in your practice. Assessment—whether based on self-reflection, peer mentoring, or a combination—will take time, especially at the beginning. Having an ongoing dialogue with your administrator may make it easier to advocate for this extra time as you can show the value of what you're doing.

Share the VPT with your administrator and explain how you use it in your planning and reflection; explain that the VPT provides a base that you use to develop early literacy–enriched storytime activities incorporating your ideas, creativity, and knowledge of your storytime community. Don't forget to share, with your administrator, the early literacy outcomes from the VPT that you are already observing in your storytime. You can talk to them about OBPE and explain how the outcomes that you are observing are linked to your storytime planning and delivery. Having these outcomes is an incredibly powerful advocacy tool that demonstrates the important work that you are doing.

You can also continue to advocate for sustained support and focus on early learning in library programs with your supervisor and colleagues. Budget constraints, staffing issues, changing leadership can all shift priorities to new directions. But your work will always matter—you have the opportunity to shape young children's lives at a critical time that comes before school starts, before formal learning. Through the magic of the games, stories, songs, and more that make up your storytimes, you are facilitating learning through play.

SHARING THE VPT

When talking to an administrator or colleague about the VPT, be sure to communicate that even though the VPT covers early literacy, it is a guide, not a comprehensive early literacy resource. Also, remember that the VPT covers only early literacy, so it cannot help you to capture information on all the learning that is taking place in your storytime. However, you can work to communicate all the different types of learning that your storytime features.

NOTES

1. Eliza T. Dresang, Melissa Gross, and Leslie Edmonds Holt, *Dynamic Youth Services through Outcome-Based Planning and Evaluation* (Chicago: American Library Association, 2006).
2. Ibid, 11.

THE FUTURE OF EARLY LEARNING AND STORYTIMES

I really appreciate our continued focus on early literacy and on encouraging play during storytime. I've been doing storytime for over twenty years, and to see how it has evolved is just mind-boggling for me. And I get excited—because I'm probably going to be retiring in the next six or more years—but I'm really excited about the future of storytimes and how the librarians are thinking outside the box, and presenting storytimes and other programs that we would not have done, even thought about in the past. I think it's an exciting new way to go.

—VIEWS2 participant

MOVING BEYOND VIEWS2

AT THE WRITING OF THIS BOOK, THE JOURNEY OF THE VIEWS2 research study has come to an end, as the grant was completed in September 2015. However, many exciting events are already taking place that will lead this work in new directions.

FOR PRACTICE

You have likely heard of OCLC—the Online Computer Library Center. OCLC is a global library cooperative that provides shared technology services, original research, and community programs for its membership and the library community at large. In 2014, OCLC received a National Leadership Grant from the Institute of Museum and Library Services (IMLS) to increase awareness and adoption of the VIEWS2 work, applying the research through the creation of online communities of practice and providing early literacy orientation to public library participants at WebJunction.org. This program, called Supercharged Storytimes, was first piloted with eighty-eight participants in Washington State in spring 2015, thus incorporating and benefiting from the input, expertise, and guidance of many of the librarians who took part in the research study. In the fall of 2015, the program was offered to over 450 public library practitioners in five other states across the country: Maine, Minnesota, Montana, North Carolina, and Wisconsin. This provided an excellent opportunity to bring research-based early literacy resources to the larger library community and more quickly impact and enhance practice. We hope these initial offerings will grow into a larger, sustained movement of communities of practice focused on providing and strengthening early literacy storytimes that build critical skills for young children.

FOR RESEARCH

We are excited about the research opportunities that can grow from this groundbreaking work. VIEWS2 has laid a foundation on which we can build future studies. The project demonstrated that the early literacy focus of public library storytimes does make a difference with children's early literacy skills while attending storytime. However, we all know that there is more to storytime than early literacy, and more to children's services than just storytime. We also know that children need to be exposed to additional skills beyond early literacy to prepare them for school and lifelong learning, and that the public library is an informal learning environment perfect for supporting these skills. Therefore, we see VIEWS2 as a beginning of a rich body of research that looks more deeply at assessment and media mentorship; begins to measure STEM and other kinds of learning taking place in storytimes and other programs; and works to understand how libraries are reaching and encouraging learning for underserved children and youth, as well as many other areas. Building this body of research will help demonstrate the value the public library brings to the children in every community.

Because VIEWS2 was developed and carried out in partnership with so many practitioners, the research has always been firmly rooted in and had strong relationships with practice. The research was heavily informed by practice, and now the research is informing practice. As we look to the future, we hope to continue this practice-to-research-to-practice cycle by consulting with practitioners from the beginning of the research process. We hope that the research-practice partnership will continue to strengthen and provide both parties with valuable information that can lead to effective practices.

BEFORE YOU GO

Storytime is one of the most rewarding parts of my job, and the more I learn about it, the more I want to keep learning. I think it's so powerful to become an expert in this field as a children's librarian. Storytime is a great experience for families, and they love it. I think the more I can be passionate about storytime, the better for everyone—because if I'm not enjoying it, that's going to show.

—VIEWS2 participant

OW THAT YOU'VE READ ABOUT AND EXPLORED THE VIEWS2 research, the VPT, and our preliminary findings and recommendations around storytime assessment, what's your next step?

In the training we provided for the librarians in the VIEWS2 study, we emphasized the importance of trying out some of these behaviors a little at a time. Supercharging your storytimes doesn't happen overnight! We know you are busy, and you may already have your own routines in place. We encourage you to think about your programming schedule, your community, and your own goals for your practice. What makes the most sense for you and your resources? How do you see this program fitting into your workflow?

One approach might be to think about the next storytime you're planning and delivering. How do *intentionality*, *interactivity*, and *community* (the three pillars of the VIEWS2 research) fit into that process?

Ask yourself:

- What is my plan for that storytime?
- How can I be *intentional* about incorporating some behaviors from the VIEWS2 early literacy domains into the activities I design around the ECRR practices?
- What early literacy outcomes am I looking for in my storytime?

- How might I be *interactive* and engage with the children and parents or caregivers during my storytime?
- How can I draw on the expertise and collegiality of my *community* of peers?
- What impact is the early literacy focus of my supercharged storytimes having on the children and parents/caregivers who make up the community I serve?
- How can I articulate to my community at large and to my community partners how my supercharged storytimes support early literacy, strengthening their children's ability to enter school ready to learn to read?

Once you've answered these questions, take a look at the reflection worksheets for the practices you covered. What went really well for you? What could you strengthen for next time? By reviewing your worksheets, you can plan, deliver, and reflect on early literacy–infused, supercharged storytimes that will provide the children with lots of fun, engaging opportunities to learn and grow. Remember, you know your practice and your community. The Supercharged approach will bolster you and give you new ways to develop your practice. In turn, you have tools and information that you can use to advocate with your administration and your community for the important work that all children's librarians and storytime providers do for the children you serve.

SUPERCHARGED STORYTIMES—COMMUNITIES OF PRACTICE

We encourage you to build your own community of practice by finding other storytime providers in your library system or geographic area. A few library systems in Washington State are building their own communities of practice around storytime. They are simply finding time to meet with each other and to focus solely on storytime practices during those meetings. If you are in a library system, talk to your supervisor about making time at the children's services meetings for a conversation focused on storytime practices. Find regular times to meet—even if it's virtually—and work through this guide and other storytime books together. Talk about storytime activities and provide feedback to one another. Support each other, because you and your peers are the best resources that you have for supercharging your storytimes.

A CELEBRATION OF STORYTIMES

In the course of the Project VIEWS2 Storytime Study, thirty-five student researchers:

- traveled 24,000 miles,
- observed 240 storytimes,
- observed forty storytime providers,
- observed more than 2,800 children,

- spent more than seven hundred hours coding storytimes, and
- watched six hundred books read in storytime.

So we've seen many kinds of storytimes in big, medium, and small libraries all over Washington State. We learned from all of these incredible storytime providers, whose patience, inspiration, and dedication show through in the children they serve and the programs they deliver. Each provider had his or her own style, personality, and approach, but they all had the common goal of helping children be better citizens of the world and lifelong learners.

We wanted to end this book by sharing with you the magic that makes up the incredible variety, creativity, and sheer fun of early literacy storytimes for young children. See figure 10.1 for just a few pieces we observed.

You brought stories to life and led kids in lively dancing, and engaging conversations. Singing at the top of their lungs, kids wriggled and chatted and played. Parents and caregivers guided and learned along with their children in storytime after storytime after storytime. There were so many different and distinct styles and personalities in the storytimes we observed—all with the common goal of helping children and their families be better citizens of the world and become lifelong learners.

We asked the librarians we interviewed for this book to share with us their favorite things about storytime. Here's what they said!

Figure 10.1

Word Cloud of Things Observed

My favorite thing about storytime is the moment when a kid makes a genuine connection to a book we're reading. Whether it's a particularly insightful question, a giggle at a joke they didn't understand before we discussed why it was funny, or a declaration of how the character in the book's experience relates to their own life experience, every time a story sparks understanding or joy, I am a happy librarian.

—*Sara Lachman*

My favorite thing about storytime is the amazing sense of community and connection that develops as I spend time reading, singing, and playing with a group of storytime kids and adults.

—*Mari Nowitz*

My favorite parts of storytime are sharing my love of reading and books and introducing rhymes, songs, games, and tales to little ones.

—*Gailene Hooper*

My favorite thing about storytime? Well, the children, of course!

—*Susan Anderson-Newham*

My favorite thing about storytime is being able to turn kids on to the joy of books. Sharing that is priceless!"

—*Bonnie Anderson*

What are your favorite things about storytime? Why do you do what you do?

We hope that through this book, we have given you a guide by which you can enhance the great work you're already doing, find new ideas and approaches to try, and use this research to advocate for the great impact you're having on your community. Supercharged storytimes come from supercharged storytime providers—that's you!

APPENDIX A
Storytime Assessment Worksheets

WE HAVE INCLUDED SEVERAL WORKSHEETS FOR YOU TO USE IN your assessment process. Please keep in mind that what works for one library may not work for another, so revise the worksheets to best suit your needs.

SELF-REFLECTION

1. **Ongoing Outcome-Based Planning and Self-Reflection Worksheet**
   This can be used with the VPT in your initial planning and then regularly throughout your storytime series to facilitate regular self-reflection.
2. **Long-Term Self-Reflection Worksheet**
   This can be used at the end of your storytime series to help you reflect on your practice and plan for the next series.

PEER MENTORING

We have included three worksheets to help you develop your own peer mentoring process. Feel free to use the first worksheet in its entirety; it is based on the VIEWS2 research. The following two worksheets are examples of the forms used by Carroll County (Washington) Public Library and Pierce County (Washington) Library System to support their peer mentoring systems. We provide these to help you understand how other library systems are supporting their process. As you work to design your peer mentoring process, you may want to borrow from all three forms to create your own.

1. **VIEWS2 Peer Mentoring Worksheet**
   This is a worksheet guideline, built from the information gathered in the interviews and informal conversations we've conducted with librarians and library administrators. We encourage you to tailor this worksheet to meet the needs of your own community and library.

2. **Carroll County Peer Coaching Forms**

   These are examples of the worksheets that Carroll County uses in their peer mentoring process. Just as a reminder, the long-observation form is used with new staff initially, and the short observation form is used with all staff.

3. **Pierce County Peer Coaching Report Form**

   This is an example of the worksheet that Pierce County uses in their peer mentoring process. The peer observers use it to record notes after they complete the observation.

ONGOING OUTCOME-BASED PLANNING AND SELF-REFLECTION WORKSHEET

Planning

1. What is the target age range of my storytimes?

2. What activities do I plan to include?

3. What early literacy outcomes from the VPT do I want to focus on?

4. Which early literacy outcomes from the VPT do I want to see in the children who attend my storytimes?

5. How do I plan to be interactive in my storytime activities?

6. How do I plan to talk with parents/caregivers and model ways to promote their children's early literacy?

7. How do I plan to incorporate fun throughout my storytime?

ONGOING OUTCOME-BASED PLANNING AND SELF-REFLECTION WORKSHEET

Self-Reflection

1. What successes did I see in my storytime?

   _____
   _____
   _____

2. Did I incorporate the early literacy content that I had planned to incorporate?

   _____
   _____
   _____

3. How did it go? Were there unexpected events that helped or hindered my delivery of early literacy content in my storytime?

   _____
   _____
   _____

4. What early literacy outcome(s) did I see in the children's behaviors? Of those, which ones did I plan for?

   _____
   _____
   _____

5. How effectively did I convey ways to support early literacy skill(s) and practices to parents/caregivers?

   _____
   _____
   _____

6. Which part(s) of my storytime do I want to reflect on and improve?

   _____
   _____
   _____

7. What early literacy content do I want to focus on in my next storytime?

   _____
   _____
   _____

8. Which outcomes would I like to see in the children's behaviors in my next storytime?

   _____
   _____
   _____

Long-Term Self-Reflection Worksheet

1. What were my initial goals for my storytimes? How did I meet those goals?

   _____

   _____

2. How did I plan and deliver my storytimes to fit the age group(s) of children who attended?

   _____

   _____

3. What early literacy domains did I focus on in my storytime series?

   _____

   _____

4. Broadly, what early literacy outcomes did I observe in the children that I want to highlight?

   _____

   _____

5. What other successes did I observe in the children that I want to highlight?

   _____

   _____

6. How effectively did I convey ways to support early literacy skill(s) and practices to parents/caregivers?

   _____

   _____

7. What do I want to tell others about my storytimes?

   _____

   _____

8. What new things do I want to try in my storytime planning?

   _____

   _____

9. Broadly, what early literacy domains and outcomes would I like to focus on in my next storytime series?

   _____

   _____

   _____

10. How will I continue to encourage a love of reading in my storytimes?

   _____

   _____

   _____

   _____

VIEWS2 Peer Mentoring Worksheet

1. What was the targeted age range of the storytime that I observed?

   _____

2. What kinds of activities were included?

   _____

   _____

3. What did I think went well in this storytime?

   _____

   _____

4. What early literacy content was emphasized by the storytime provider?

   _____

   _____

5. What early literacy outcomes did I observe in the children's behaviors?

   _____

   _____

6. Did the provider and the families enjoy the storytime? What reactions did I observe in the children and parents/caregivers who attended?

   _____

   _____

7. What are some anecdotes and examples of meaningful interactions between the provider and the children and parents/caregivers?

   _____

   _____

8. What are some recommendations for how to continue to promote early literacy in the next storytime?

   _____

   _____

9. How did the provider encourage enjoyment of books and language activities during the storytime?

   _____

   _____

10. What storytime elements do I want to borrow and use in my own storytimes?

    _____

    _____

> ❿ We recommend using a combination of peer mentoring (to build community and collegiality among peers) and self-reflection (to encourage continual growth and improvement).

CARROLL COUNTY PEER COACHING—SAMPLE LONG-OBSERVATION FORM

Name: _____

Peer Observed: _____

Date: _____

Directions: Complete this form for each peer coaching observation to share in your reflection conference.

Physical Surroundings

Are the storytime participants sitting comfortably with a clear view of the storytime presenter? Are books, easels, props, etc., displayed so that all participants can see?
Give a brief description of the physical surroundings, along with any suggestions for change.

_____

_____

_____

_____

_____

Storytime Content / Presentation

Are books and activities age appropriate for the participants? Were they presented in an engaging manner?
Jot down a comment about the match between the books and activities and the age of the children, along with any suggestions for more appropriate alternatives. Add a comment about presentation skills, e.g., " Changed voice for characters and kept the children amused."

_____

_____

_____

_____

_____

Are emergent literacy concepts reinforced throughout the storytime, as described in the Storytime Planning Sheets and other Toolkit resources?
List concepts you observe being reinforced, and briefly describe how they were reinforced in the storytime, e.g., "Concepts about print—reinforced by pointing out title and author." Jot down any ideas you may have for reinforcing additional concepts throughout the storytime.

_____

_____

_____

_____

_____

CARROLL COUNTY PEER COACHING—SAMPLE
LONG-OBSERVATION FORM (Continued)

Engagement of Storytime Participants

Is the pacing or flow of the storytime activities working well? Do you see a variety of books and activities that fit the theme and/or age group and engage the children? Is the transition between activities smooth?
Jot down a few notes about the pacing or flow of the storytime activities, along with any suggestions you think of for the variety of books and activities and/or transition times.

_____

_____

_____

_____

_____

Are the children actively engaged at different points throughout the storytime? If the parents/caregivers are present, are they engaged with their child?
List the types of engagement you observe throughout the storytime, along with any suggestions you think of to encourage more active participation.

_____

_____

_____

_____

_____

Appropriate Behavior of Participants during Storytime

Are management techniques being used effectively throughout the storytime so that everyone is enjoying the experience? Are both children and adults behaving appropriately?
Give a general description of participant behavior during the storytime, along with any suggestions for encouraging appropriate behavior from children and/or adults.

_____

_____

_____

_____

—ELAINE M. CZARNECKI 1/07
LITERACY CONSULTANT, RESOURCES IN READING

CARROLL COUNTY PEER COACHING—SAMPLE SHORT-OBSERVATION FORM

Name: _____

Peer Observed: _____

Date: _____

Physical Surroundings

1. Children all facing you / Parents, too!
2. Comment about being comfortable set parents at ease

_____

_____

Storytime Content / Presentation

1. Loved the voice for Mrs. Tweezers, children were mesmerized!
2. Fingerplays and/or movement activity might help with fidgeting between stories . . .
3. Closing song was really cute—never heard that one before

_____

_____

Storytime Content / Emergent Literacy Concepts

1. Predicting before and during *Owen* to reinforce comprehension
2. Excellent technique of "thumbs up, thumbs down" to involve all of the children
3. Sticky notes worked great for predicting points
4. Reinforced vocabulary development with the word "binoculars"—was perfect to have the prop and pass it around!

_____

_____

Engagement / Behavior of Storytime Participants

1. Children engaged and attentive during stories
2. Parents had a few side conversations, but they stopped when you shared why you were asking the children to make predictions—some even gave you the thumbs up, thumbs down too! Did you ever try asking them at the beginning to model appropriate responses with you?

_____

_____

—ELAINE M. CZARNECKI 1/07
LITERACY CONSULTANT, RESOURCES IN READING

PIERCE COUNTY PEER COACHING REPORT FORM

1. Person Observed:

   _____
   _____
   _____

2. Type of Storytime:

   _____
   _____
   _____

3. Books Shared:

   _____
   _____
   _____

4. Singing:

   _____
   _____
   _____

5. Reading:

   _____
   _____
   _____

6. Writing:

   _____
   _____
   _____

7. Playing:

   _____
   _____
   _____

8. The one idea that I would like to *steal*:

   _____
   _____
   _____
   _____
   _____
   _____
   _____

APPENDIX B
VIEWS2/Head Start Crosswalk

ABOUT THE CROSSWALK BETWEEN THE VPT AND THE HEAD START EARLY LEARNING OUTCOMES FRAMEWORK

One way that you can articulate to your supervisors, administrators, and partners how you are supporting early literacy development in your supercharged storytimes is by providing a crosswalk: a comparison of the terms and content of the domains used by the library and other educational groups such as Head Start, child care early learning programs, the state Department of Education, and home visiting programs, to name a few.

In this appendix, we provide a crosswalk from the VPT to Head Start's *Early Learning Outcomes Framework: Ages Birth to Five.*[1] By following the process we did for producing the crosswalk for Head Start, you can create your own crosswalk with your state's early learning standards.

Let's say that you have used the VPT domains to show how your programs and/or other services support early literacy. You can now use those connections to help other agencies understand how you support early literacy by using your partners' terminology. This can be done for your own state early learning guidelines. We are using Head Start as our example because it is national. For Head Start, we began with the VPT examples for children in each domain in column 1. Then we looked at the sections entitled Language and Communication (for infants, toddlers, and preschoolers) and Literacy (for preschoolers) areas of *Head Start Early Learning Outcomes Framework: Ages Birth to Five.*

Under each of these domains, there are goals listed and numbered, with descriptions of developmental progressions and indicators about children's knowledge and behavior at each age level. These offer more detailed insights under each goal. By comparing the child behaviors under each VPT domain with the behaviors noted under each goal, we filled in the second column.

You may have already used your own state's early learning guidelines as a way to communicate with partners and to advocate for the library in the world of early childhood education. If so, you can use those terms in your crosswalk. If you find it useful, you can use the same method to develop crosswalks for your state's early learning guidelines. The crosswalk is a powerful tool to help all those serving young children and their families and caregivers to understand the strong role the library plays in supporting early literacy development and for library staff to articulate these connections.

NOTE

1. *Head Start Child Development and Early Learning Framework: Ages Birth to Five*, 2015, http://eclkc.ohs.acf.hhs.gov/hslc/hs/sr/approach/pdf/ohs-framework.pdf.

Crosswalk for VIEWS2 Planning Tool (VPT) and
Head Start Early Learning Outcomes Framework: Ages Birth to Five

VPT DOMAINS AND GOALS	HEAD START DOMAINS AND SUB-DOMAINS
I. Language Use: How to Use Words	**Language and Communication**
• Children use language for a variety of purposes. • Children demonstrate an understanding of language by listening.	• Attending and Understanding (B–5) • Communicating and Speaking (B–5)
II. Communication: How to Talk and Share	**Language and Communication**
• Children communicate effectively. • Children understand and use the conventions of social communication.	• Attending and Understanding (B–5) • Communicating and Speaking (B–5)
III. Phonological Awareness: Playing with Sounds	**Language and Communication**
• Children demonstrate phonological awareness.	• Emergent Literacy (B–2) • Literacy: Phonological Awareness (3–5)
IV. Vocabulary: Understanding and Using Words	**Language and Communication**
• Children use expressive vocabulary. • Children demonstrate progression in grammar and syntax.	• Communicating and Speaking (B–5) • Vocabulary (B–5)
V. Comprehension: Understanding Words, Stories, Directions, Ideas, etc.	**Language and Communication**
• Children use receptive vocabulary and comprehension. • Children demonstrate comprehension and meaning in language.	• Attending and Understanding (B–5) • Communicating and Speaking (B–5) • Vocabulary (B–5)
VI. Print Concepts: Connecting with Books and Stories	**Language and Communication**
• Children demonstrate awareness of the print concepts. • Children demonstrate comprehension of printed materials. • Children demonstrate appreciation and enjoyment of reading.	• Emergent Literacy (B–2) • Literacy: Print and Alphabet Knowledge (3–5) • Literacy: Comprehension and Text Structure (3–5)
VII. Alphabetic Knowledge: Exploring with Letters	**Language and Communication**
• Children demonstrate awareness of the alphabetic principle.	• Emergent Literacy (B–2) • Literacy: Print and Alphabet Knowledge (3–5)
VIII. Writing Concepts: Writing	**Language and Communication**
• Children demonstrate alphabetic knowledge. • Children use writing skills and demonstrate knowledge of writing conventions. • Children use writing for a variety of purposes.	• Emergent Literacy (B–2) • Literacy: Print and Alphabet Knowledge (3–5) • Literacy: Writing (3–5)

*alphabetic principle: the idea that letters and letter patterns represent the sounds of spoken language, that there are predictable relationships between sounds and letters.

VIEWS2 Domain information: http://views2.ischool.uw.edu/resources/

Head Start Early Learning Outcomes Framework information: http://eclkc.ohs.acf.hhs.gov/hslc/hs/sr/approach/pdf/ohs-framework.pdf

APPENDIX C
VPT Organized by Age

Literacy Concepts for Birth to 18 Months

VIEWS2 Valuable Initiatives in Early Learning that Work Successfully

■ Alphabetic Knowledge / Exploring with Letters

Educator/Adult	Children
Reads books with repetitive sounds and/or pronounces words deliberately and slowly when reading	Imitate sounds when looking at words in a book
Points toward a book while reading or when a book is within reach of children	Point to words in a book

■ Communication / How to Talk and Share

Educator/Adult	Children
Provides pauses so that children can interject	Vocalize/use words and gestures to solicit attention
Encourages children to imitate simple words	Imitate words (e.g., simple greetings)
Greets children with nonverbal gestures (e.g., waves hello) in order to communicate	Use nonverbal gestures for social conventions of greeting (e.g., waving goodbye)
Encourages caretakers to model eye contact and taking turns in communication as well as sounds and words one-on-one	Participate in a one-on-one conversation by making sounds or sometimes using words

■ Comprehension / Understanding Words, Stories, Directions, Ideas, etc.

Educator/Adult	Children
Uses simple words to give children single-step directions (e.g., "Please bring me the ball") or indirect invitations (e.g., "Let's listen") and provides time for them to respond (e.g., "Clap," children clap)	Respond appropriately to familiar words (e.g., "Clap," children clap)
	Follow single-step directions (e.g., bringing the ball when asked)
	Have a receptive vocabulary of more than fifty words in home language
Asks children simple questions that can be answered with gestures toward a particular person (e.g., "Where is Mommy?") or object (e.g., "Where is your blanket?")	Point to familiar person(s) when requested
	Point to objects when named (e.g., pointing to blanket when asked, "Where is your blanket?")
Directs children's attention using visual gaze and/or gestures	Pay attention to what the speaker is looking at or pointing to

▪ Language Use / How to Use Words

Educator/Adult	Children
Provides or recites oral stories (e.g., nursery rhymes) to children in order to prompt them to express simple thoughts or ideas	Enjoy listening to oral stories
	Use single words to express thoughts and ideas (e.g., when seeing the sun, saying "sun")

▪ Phonological Awareness / Playing with Sounds

Educator/Adult	Children
Reads to children from books with developmentally appropriate content, and pauses to provide them time to insert the sounds of familiar words	Vocalize familiar words when read to
Uses rhymes in stories, greetings, and directions	Recite the last word of familiar rhymes, with assistance

▪ Print Concepts / Connecting with Books and Stories

Educator/Adult	Children
Highlights and points to pictures or words in a book, spaces between words, or words representing pictured objects	Pay attention to pictures or words in books
Prompts children to point to pictures, characters, or objects in books	Point to familiar pictures, characters, and objects in books
Presents children with the opportunity to explore books (e.g., what is on the pages) as part of hands-on activity	Explore books (e.g., flipping or turning through pages)

▪ Vocabulary / Understanding and Using Words

Educator/Adult	Children
Uses gestures in combination with words when communicating	Combine words and gestures (e.g., waving when saying goodbye)
Invites children to label familiar objects in books or in the environment	Use eight to ten understandable words (e.g., *daddy*, *bottle*, *up*)
Presents children with the opportunity to label aspects of people, places, and events	Use short telegraphic sentences (e.g., "Me go" or "There Mama.")

▪ Writing Concepts / Writing

Educator/Adult	Children
Asks children to point out words and pictures in a book in order to prompt them to think about the differences between words and pictures	Point to words in a book
	Imitate other person's writing, drawing, or scribbling by making their own marks or scribbles
Demonstrates making marks on a page in front of children	Scribble spontaneously

Adult component (PET) by E. Feldman, E. Dresang, K. Burnett, J. Capps, and K. Campana. Children's component (BCPAF) by E. Feldman.

Literacy Concepts for 18 to 36 Months

VIEWS2 <small>Valuable Initiatives in Early Learning that Work Successfully</small>

■ Alphabetic Knowledge / Exploring with Letters

Educator/Adult	Children
Prompts children to recite or sing the letters of the alphabet	Recite a song with letters of the alphabet, with assistance (e.g., the alphabet song or a recitation)
Asks children to point to print on the page of a picture book or other illustrated page, poster, etc.	Begin to understand that print represents words (e.g., pretending to read text)

■ Communication / How to Talk and Share

Educator/Adult	Children
Responds to children's use of appropriate cues to solicit attention	Address listener appropriately to get attention (e.g., when speaking to another child, using that child's name)
Prompts children to use adjectives to describe things or events in order to communicate effectively	Uses adjectives to describe a thing or event (e.g., "big toy," "fun ride")
Provides children with the opportunity to use sound effects to convey meaning (e.g., "crash," "bang," "buzz," animal sounds)	Use sound effects in play
Provides children with the opportunity to participate in turn-taking conversations (e.g., "What did you like about the book?")	Begin to demonstrate taking turns in conversation

■ Comprehension / Understanding Words, Stories, Directions, Ideas, etc.

Educator/Adult	Children
Prompts children to identify different body parts by pointing	Identify at least three body parts, when requested
Prompts children to identify people, objects, or actions by name (e.g., "Who is this?" "What is this a picture of?" "What is this person doing?")	Identify some people, objects, and actions by name
Asks children simple questions (e.g., "Do you see birds in the trees around your house?") and pauses, allowing children time to respond	Answer simple questions with words or gestures
Provides experiences that prompt children to ask questions or reflect some knowledge of events/phenomena	Ask questions that demonstrate knowledge of events or phenomena (e.g., "Why did the boy run away?" "How did the water turn blue?")

■ Language Use / How to Use Words

Educator/Adult	Children
Prompts children to recount events	Recount an event, with assistance
Prompts children to reflect on the sequence of events in an orally narrated story	Begin to follow the sequence of events in an orally narrated story
Provides opportunity for fingerplay (e.g., songs and games that use hand and finger gestures)	Enjoy fingerplay (e.g., songs and games that use hand and finger gestures)
Prompts children to point to objects within the pages of a book or within given context	Attempt to locate objects that are discussed by others

■ Phonological Awareness / Playing with Sounds

Educator/Adult	Children
Uses reading style (e.g., pauses, providing children time to respond) where children can say the last word of familiar rhymes/songs	Complete a familiar rhyme or fingerplay by providing the last word
Invites children to act out a variety of tempos or speeds of sounds (e.g., clapping hands rapidly and then slowly; speaking rapidly and then slowly)	Imitate tempo and speed of sound

■ Print Concepts / Connecting with Books and Stories

Educator/Adult	Children
Prompts children to recall specific characters from age-appropriate stories	Recall specific characters or actions from familiar stories
Inserts pauses, providing children time to respond, and asks questions during story reading that allow children to make predictions	Anticipate what comes next in known stories, with assistance (e.g., predicting the next animal in an animal concept book)
Prompts children to respond to the emotional experiences or expressions of characters in books	Respond to emotional expressions in a book (e.g., pointing to a happy face)
Invites children to make comments on books read recently or in the past	Make comments on book

■ Vocabulary / Understanding and Using Words

Educator/Adult	Children
Introduces unfamiliar objects and prompts children to request labels from caregiver	Ask others to label unfamiliar objects
Uses simple three- to four-word sentences (with mostly one- to two-syllable words) at least twice, followed by a pause so children can imitate	Imitate simple two-word phrase/sentence
Provides experiences that prompt children to ask questions	Use simple questions in speech, but may not use correct grammar
Invites children to use adjectives to describe objects or things described in stories	Use adjectives in phrases (e.g., "big bag," "green bear")

■ Writing Concepts / Writing

Educator/Adult	Children
Asks children about attempts to produce written, age-appropriate material (e.g., scribbles)	Scribble and make marks on paper purposefully
Uses hand to point out words as they are read	Demonstrate an understanding that we hear and see words by pointing randomly to text while it is being read out loud (i.e., that a spoken word is also represented in print)
Provides writing explorations related to fine motor skills, gross motor skills, and postural control	Draw horizontal and vertical lines

Adult component (PET) by E. Feldman, E. Dresang, K. Burnett, J. Capps, and K. Campana. Children's component (BCPAF) by E. Feldman.

Literacy Concepts for 36 to 60 Months

VIEWS2 Valuable Initiatives in Early Learning that Work Successfully

■ Alphabetic Knowledge / Exploring with Letters

Educator/Adult	Children
Points out shapes with specific letters	Associate the names of letters with their shapes
Prompts children to match letters and sounds	Correctly identify ten or more letters of the alphabet
Prompts children to think about how letters and numbers are different	
Points to each word separately while reading	
Prompts children to identify the same word across pages of a book	

■ Communication / How to Talk and Share

Educator/Adult	Children
Solicits use of words, signs, or picture books to state points of view, likes/dislikes, and opinions; does not include questions with a "right" answer	State point of view, likes/dislikes, and opinions using words, signs, or picture books
Encourages children to pay attention through positive feedback	Pay attention to speaker during conversation
Points out facial expressions of characters in stories or encourages children to make their own facial expression to express emotions	Begin to demonstrate understanding of nonverbal cues (e.g., recognizing or making facial expressions for pride)

■ Comprehension / Understanding Words, Stories, Directions, Ideas, etc.

Educator/Adult	Children
Contrasts real and made-up words to prompt children to talk about the differences between words that are real and made up	Distinguish between real and made-up words
Asks questions to elicit short verbal answers *or* gestures that demonstrate that children are following the story/activity/conversation	Respond to questions with verbal answers or gestures
Uses strategies to assist children in having a conversation by extending/expanding thoughts or ideas expressed by others in regards to a story, book, or song (e.g., "I hear that you think the bunny is pretending the box is a car. Who else has an idea about what the bunny is doing? What type of car is it?")	Extend/expand on a thought or idea expressed by another
	Engage in conversation that develops a thought or idea (e.g., telling about a past event)

■ Language Use / How to Use Words

Educator/Adult	Children
Asks questions about a recent event	Recount some details of a recent event
Encourages children to identify animals and invites personification (e.g., making animal sounds, moving like an animal)	Mimic animal sounds
Asks questions about specific details and events in a story and provides positive feedback when children recall details	Respond to questions with appropriate answers

■ Phonological Awareness / Playing with Sounds

Educator/Adult	Children
Reinforces recognition of beginning word sounds (e.g., "*Book* begins with the *b* sound.")	Identify initial sound of words, with assistance
Encourages children to find multiple objects in a picture with the same beginning sound	Find objects in a picture with the same beginning sound, with assistance
Points out the differences between similar-sounding words (e.g., *three* and *tree*)	Differentiate between similar-sounding words

■ Print Concepts / Connecting with Books and Stories

Educator/Adult	Children
Points to letters in the text and asks children to identify them	Identify some individual letters in the text
Points out signs and symbols in the environment when reading picture books. Asks children if they've seen these before (e.g., "On your way to the library, did you stop at a light? Was it a red light like this one?")	Recognize some signs and symbols in the environment (e.g., stop sign or traffic light)
Asks children, "Do you have a favorite book? What's the title?"	Express the title of a favorite book

■ Vocabulary / Understanding and Using Words

Educator/Adult	Children
Models using multiple words to explain ideas (e.g., "Another way of saying that is . . .", defining a new concept/idea)	Use multiple words to explain ideas (e.g., when talking about being mad, saying "angry," "frustrated," etc.)
Ask children to talk about how they feel about what is happening in the story	Use words to express emotions (e.g., *happy, sad, tired, scared*)
Prompts children to share stories about/describe their preferences and previous experiences, then assists in putting in sequence (e.g., "Oh, you have also gone to a grocery store. What did you do when you got there first? Did you get a cart? What happened next?")	Describe a task, project, and/or event sequentially in three or more sentences

■ **Writing Concepts / Writing**

Educator/Adult	Children
Incorporates drawing into storytime activities	Begin to draw representational figures
Prompts children to find the same letter in different media (e.g., book, poster, sign)	Identify letters to match the said-aloud letter name
Provides activities that encourage drawing basic geometric shapes	Draw basic geometric shapes (e.g., circle, triangle)
Provides activities that encourage pretend writing	Use pretend writing activities during play to show print conventions in primary language
Invites children to make up and tell stories and write them out	Talk aloud about creative ideas and stories and ask adults to write them out
Invites children to work together to make up a poem and writes it out	Ask adults to write out rhymes to make a simple poem

Adult component (PET) by E. Feldman, E. Dresang, K. Burnett, J. Capps, and K. Campana. Children's component (BCPAF) by E. Feldman.

VIEWS2 GLOSSARY OF TERMS

AK. alphabetic knowledge

ALA. American Library Association

ALSC. Association for Library Service to Children

BCPAF. Benchmarks for Curriculum Planning and Assessment Framework (developed by Dr. Erika Feldman)

ECRR. Every Child Ready to Read 1, 2

ELPLP. Early Learning Public Library Partnership

ELSA. Early Literacy Skills Assessment

IMLS. Institute of Museum and Library Services

NELP. National Early Literacy Panel

NICHD. National Institute of Child Health and Human Development

NRP. National Reading Panel

OCLC. Online Computer Library Center (formerly Ohio College Library Center)

PA. phonological awareness

PET. Program Evaluation Tool (developed by Dr. Erika Feldman, Dr. Eliza Dresang, Dr. Kathleen Burnett, Dr. Janet Capps, and Kathleen Campana)

PLA. Public Library Association

VIEWS. Valuable Initiatives in Early Learning that Work Successfully

WAKIDS. Washington Kindergarten Inventory of Developing Skills

WLA. Washington Library Association

WLMA. Washington Library Media Association

WSL. Washington State Library

INDEX

A

action songs, 69, 71, 92
active play, 76
activities, examples of, 78–83, 93–97, 99–100
administrators, communicating with, 131
advocacy, 120, 125–126, 131
age ranges, adapting storytimes to, 10–11, 40,
    55, 69, 84, 98
alike and different, concept of, 38, 100
alphabetic knowledge
    as early literacy domain, 10, 17–18*f*
    playing and, 83
    reading and, 52–53
    singing and, 67
    talking and, 38
    VPT charts for, 28*f*, 155, 157, 159
    writing and, 94–96
Anderson, Bonnie, 89–98, 101n1, 140
Anderson-Newham, Susan, 75–78, 81, 83–84,
    86n1, 140
"Apples and Bananas" song, 65, 66
assessment
    case studies of, 118–123
    vs. evaluation, 108, 125–127
    incorporating into storytime practice,
        125–131
    overview of, 105, 107–109
    peer mentoring as, 108–109, 117–123,
        125–131
    self-reflection as, 108–109, 111–116,
        125–131
    VIEWS2 study on, 107–109, 113–115,
        117–118, 123
    worksheets for, 141–150

B

babies. *See* children ages birth to 18 months
background knowledge, 18*f*, 19
Becker, Bonny, 35, 49
Bergquist, Greta, 121
"BINGO" song, 64, 67
Birds dramatic play activity, 79–80
block play, 81, 84

"Bluebird, Bluebird" song, 69, 79–80
Book Babies book sets, 53
books
    babies' interaction with, 37, 53
    enjoyment of, 27
    examples with, 35, 47, 49–51, 54, 58
    questions about, 46
boxes, story play, 80–81
Brunson, Ericka, 105, 121–123, 130

C

cameras, in assessment, 113–114
caregivers, sharing tips with, 12–13, 40, 55–56,
    69–70, 84, 98
Carroll County Public Library, 118–119, 122,
    141–142, 147–149
case studies, 118–123
CATE model, 126–127
children ages birth to 18 months
    alphabetic knowledge in, 28, 38, 53, 67, 155
    charts for, 155–156
    communication and, 22, 33, 49, 63, 155
    comprehension in, 26, 37, 51, 66, 155
    language use and, 23, 34, 50, 64, 156
    phonological awareness in, 24, 35, 50, 64,
        156
    playing and, 79–80, 83, 85
    print awareness in, 57
    print concepts and, 27, 37, 52, 66, 155
    reading and, 37, 49–58
    singing and, 62, 63–68, 71
    talking and, 32, 33–39, 41
    vocabulary and, 25, 35–36, 51, 57, 65, 156
    writing and, 29, 39, 54, 68, 95, 99, 101, 156
children ages 18 to 36 months
    alphabetic knowledge in, 28, 38, 53, 67, 157
    charts for, 157–158
    communication and, 22, 34, 49, 63, 157
    comprehension in, 26, 37, 52, 66, 157
    language use and, 23, 34, 50, 64, 157
    phonological awareness in, 24, 35, 50, 65,
        158

children ages 18 to 36 months (*continued*)
    playing and, 78–85
    print awareness in, 57
    print concepts and, 27, 37–38, 52, 67, 158
    singing and, 63–68, 71
    talking and, 34–41
    vocabulary and, 25, 36, 51, 57–58, 65, 158
    writing and, 29, 39, 54, 68, 98–101, 158
children ages 36 to 60 months
    alphabetic knowledge in, 28, 38, 53, 67, 94, 96, 159
    charts for, 159–161
    communication and, 22, 34, 49, 63, 159
    comprehension in, 26, 37, 52, 66, 159
    language use and, 23, 34, 50, 64, 160
    phonological awareness in, 24, 35, 50, 65, 160
    playing and, 78–79, 80–85
    print awareness in, 57
    print concepts and, 27, 38, 52, 67, 160
    reading and, 46, 49–55, 57–58
    singing and, 63–68, 71
    talking and, 34–39, 41
    vocabulary and, 25, 36, 51, 58, 65, 160
    writing and, 29, 39, 54, 68, 90, 93–97, 99–101, 161
Children's Access to Technology Evaluation (CATE), 126–127
coaching. *See* peer mentoring
communication
    as early literacy domain, 10, 17–18*f*
    playing and, 79, 81
    reading and, 49
    singing and, 63
    talking and, 33–34
    VPT charts for, 22*f*, 155, 157, 159
    writing and, 97
community building, xv, 6, 9, 121–122, 137–138
    See also peer mentoring
comprehension
    as early literacy domain, 10, 17–18*f*
    playing and, 79, 82
    reading and, 51–52
    singing and, 66
    talking and, 36–37
    VPT charts for, 26*f*, 155, 157, 159
    writing and, 94
constructive play, 76
conversational storytimes, 33
cortisol study, 62
craft time, 90–93, 96–97, 98, 100–101
crosswalks
    VIEWS2 *vs.* ECRR, 18*f*
    VPT *vs.* Head Start Early Learning Outcomes, 151–153

D

decoding, 38, 56–57, 62
Delavan, Erica, 7

Developmentally Appropriate Play (Gaye), 86
Dewdney, Anna, 58
dialogic reading, 46–48
director role, 76
domains, early literacy, 10–11, 17–18*f*
    See also specific domains
dramatic play, 76, 78–79, 85
Dresang, Eliza T., x, 9, 125, 126
Dynamic Youth Services through Outcome-Based Planning and Evaluation, 125–127

E

Early Learning Public Library Partnership (ELPLP), ix
early literacy
    domains of, 10–11, 17–18*f*
    ECRR skills and practices of, 18–19
    incorporating into storytimes, 5–13
early literacy storytimes. *See* storytimes, early literacy
evaluation *vs.* assessment, 108, 125–127
Every Child Ready to Read 1st ed. (ECRR1), 17–20
Every Child Ready to Read 2nd ed. (ECRR2), 6, 17–20, 32, 48, 77, 91

F

feedback, peer. *See* peer mentoring
fine motor skills, 71, 89–92, 95, 100–101
fingerplays, 61–62, 64, 71, 92, 139*f*
flannelboards, 66–67, 99, 100
Fleming, Denise, 38, 50
forms. *See* worksheets
fun, importance of, 13, 49
functional play, 76

G

games, 55, 100
grammar and syntax, 25*f*
Gray, Colette, 8, 115
Gronlund, Gaye, 86
Gross, Melissa, 125, 126
gross motor skills, 68, 71, 89, 92, 95, 100–101

H

handwriting. *See* writing
Head Start Early Learning Outcomes Framework, 151–153
"Hickety, Pickety, Bumblebee" song, 99
"The Hokey-Pokey" song, 65, 68
Holt, Leslie Edmonds, 125, 126
Hooper, Gailene, 1, 61, 63, 68–70, 71n1, 140

I

I Stink! (McMullan), 35, 47
In the Small, Small Pond (Fleming), 38, 50
infants. *See* children ages birth to 18 months
Institute of Museum and Library Services (IMLS), ix, 135
intentionality, xv, 6–7, 12, 114–116, 127, 137

interactivity
    overview of, xv, 6, 7–8
    playing and, 83
    reading and, 45–46, 54
    singing and, 68
    talking and, 39
    writing and, 97
Internet resources, 4, 21
iPads, as music players, 70
"Itsy Bitsy Spider" song, 64, 68, 69, 71, 92

K

Keats, Ezra Jack, 35
Kitsap Regional Library, 121–122

L

Lachman, Sara, 31–33, 39–40, 42n1, 54, 140
language use
    as early literacy domain, 10, 17–18*f*
    playing and, 80, 82
    reading and, 49–50
    singing and, 64
    talking and, 34
    VPT charts for, 23*f*, 156, 157, 160
    writing and, 97
lapsit storytimes. *See* children ages birth to 18
    months
learning environments, 13, 78, 91
letter hunt activity, 95–96
letter knowledge, 18–19
    See also alphabetic knowledge
letter puzzles activity, 94, 96
letter writing, 89–90, 94–96, 99–101
librarians
    case studies with, 118–123
    community building among, 6, 9, 119–123,
        137–138
    as early learning professionals, x, 76
    tips from, 39–40, 54–56, 68–70, 81, 83–84,
        97–98, 130
    as VIEWS2 participants, xvi, 3–4
    See also storytime providers
librarianship, elevation of, x
libraries. *See* public libraries
lifelong learning, support of, 13
Llama Llama Red Pajama (Dewdney), 58

M

MacBlain, Sean, 8, 115
Making Pumpkin Pie activity, 78–79, 85
McMullan, Kate and Jim, 35, 47
mentoring. *See* peer mentoring
Moss, Elizabeth, 53
motor skills, 68, 71, 89–92, 95, 100–101

N

name recognition, 90, 92–94, 99–100
name tags, 93–94, 100
narrative skills, 18
Nelson, Judy, 15, 119–120, 122, 130

Nowitz, Mari, 45, 48–49, 53–56, 58n1, 140
Nutbrown, Cathy, 117

O

OBPE model, 126–127
observation, in assessment, 119–122, 142,
    147–150
"Old MacDonald" song, 65, 67, 70
Online Computer Library Center (OCLC), 135
onomatopoeia, 50
opening songs, 63, 99, 139*f*
oral language, 18, 23, 32, 48, 62
Outcome-Based Planning and Evaluation
    (OBPE), 126–127
outcome-based processes, 125–131, 141,
    143–144

P

parentese, 32
parents, sharing tips with, 12–13, 40, 55–56,
    69–70, 84, 98
peer mentoring
    as outcome-based process, 125–131
    overview of, 9, 108–109, 117–123
    as self-reflection counterpart, 128–129
    worksheets for, 141–142, 146–150
Peterson, Shannon, 121
phonological awareness
    as early literacy domain, 10–11*f*, 17–18
    playing and, 80, 82
    reading and, 50
    singing and, 64–65
    talking and, 34–35
    VPT charts for, 24*f*, 156, 158, 160
    writing and, 95–96
Pierce County Library System, 119–121, 122,
    142, 150
pincer grasp, 90, 92
planning. *See* VIEWS2 Planning Tool (VPT)
playing
    importance of, 77–78
    scaffolding and, 85–86
    tips on, 81, 83–84
    types of, 75–77
    VPT and, 19, 78–83
    worksheet on, 88
practices, ECRR2, 17–19
preschoolers. *See* children ages 36 to 60 months
print awareness, 18, 57
print concepts
    as early literacy domain, 10, 17–18*f*
    playing and, 82
    reading and, 52
    singing and, 66–67
    talking and, 37–38
    VPT charts for, 27*f*, 156, 158, 160
    writing and, 94
print conventions, 18*f*, 19
print motivation, 18
print referencing, 47–48

prior knowledge, 19
Project VIEWS, ix–x
Project VIEWS2, x–xi, xvii, 3–4, 5–13, 107–109, 113–115, 138–140
prompts, reading, 46
props, 85, 95
public libraries
    case studies of, 118–123
    as early learning partners, ix–xi, 3–5
    as informal learning environments, 13, 78, 91, 136
Pumpkin Pie activity, 78–79, 85

R
reading
    importance of, 48
    scaffolding and, 56–58
    techniques for, 45–48
    tips on, 54–56
    VPT and, 19, 49–54
    worksheet on, 60
repetition, 9, 36, 41, 65
research studies
    on babies' vocabulary, 36
    on early literacy storytimes, ix–x, 3–5, 107–109, 113–115, 135–136, 138–140
    on reading, 38, 46
    on scaffolding, 8
    on singing and music, 62
Rhyming Dust Bunnies (Thomas), 54
"Rum Sum Sum" song, 68

S
scaffolding
    overview of, 8–9
    playing and, 85–86
    reading and, 56–58
    singing and, 70–71
    talking and, 40–42
    writing and, 98–101
self-reflection
    as outcome-based process, 125–131
    overview of, 9, 108–109, 111–116
    as peer mentoring counterpart, 128–129
    worksheets for, 43, 60, 73, 88, 103, 141, 143–145
Sendak, Maurice, 51
shapes, activities with, 99–100
similar and different, concept of, 38, 100
singing
    importance of, 61–62
    scaffolding and, 70–71
    tips on, 68–70
    VPT and, 19, 62–68
    worksheet on, 73
skills, of ECRR1, 17–18
The Snowy Day (Keats), 35
social communication, 22

songs
    action songs, 69, 71, 92
    opening songs, 63, 99, 139*f*
    zipper songs, 70
    See also singing
stage manager role, 76
Stoltz, Dorothy, 118–119, 122, 130
story play boxes, 80–81
storytime providers
    case studies with, 118–123
    community building among, 6, 9, 119–123, 137–138
    job titles of, xvi
    See also librarians
storytimes, early literacy
    ECRR and, 17–20
    framework for, 6–13
    future of, 133, 135–136
    impact of, ix–x, xv, 5–7, 13, 107–109, 114–116, 135–136
    research on, ix–x, 3–5, 107–109, 113–115, 135–136, 138–140
structured play, 75–76, 78–80, 85
Supercharged Storytimes pilot program, x, 6, 135
Sylvan Way Library, 121–122

T
talking
    importance of, 31–32
    scaffolding and, 41–42
    tips on, 39–40
    VPT and, 19, 33–39
    worksheet on, 43
technology, in storytimes, 70, 95
themed play, 80, 82
Thomas, Jan, 54
toddlers. *See* children ages 18 to 36 months
toys, 76, 79–80, 83–84
    See also playing
training, in VIEWS2, 3–4, 6–7, 113, 120–121

U
unstructured play, 75–78, 80–83, 86

V
video cameras, in assessment, 113–114
VIEWS2 Planning Tool (VPT)
    for alphabetic knowledge, 28*f*, 38, 52–53, 67, 83, 94–96
    assessment and, 113–116, 127–128, 131
    charts for, by age level, 155–161
    for communication, 22*f*, 33–34, 49, 63, 79, 81, 97
    for comprehension, 26*f*, 36–37, 51–52, 66, 79, 82, 94
    vs. ECRR, 18*f*, 19*f*
    vs. Head Start Early Learning Outcomes, 151–153

for language use, 23*f,* 34, 49–50, 64, 80, 82, 97

overview of, 5–7, 10–13

for phonological awareness, 24*f,* 34–35, 50, 64–65, 80, 82, 96

for print concepts, 27*f,* 37–38, 52, 66–67, 82, 94

for vocabulary, 25*f,* 35–36, 50–51, 65, 79–80, 82, 96

web resources for, 21

for writing concepts, 29*f,* 39, 53–54, 67–68, 83, 94–97

VIEWS2 study, x–xi, xvii, 3–4, 5–13, 107–109, 113–115, 138–140

A Visitor for Bear (Becker), 35, 49

vocabulary

as early literacy component, 10, 17–19

playing and, 79, 80, 82

reading and, 50–51, 57–58

singing and, 65

talking and, 35–36

VPT charts for, 25*f,* 156, 158, 160

writing and, 96

VPT. *See* VIEWS2 Planning Tool (VPT)

W

Washington State Library, ix

web resources, 4, 21

Where the Wild Things Are (Sendak), 51

wiggly children, 95

word cloud, of VIEWS2 observations, 139*f*

word smushing game, 55

worksheets

for outcome-based planning, 141, 143–144

for peer mentoring, 141–142, 146–150

for self-reflection, 43, 60, 73, 88, 103, 112–113, 141, 143–145

writing

importance of, 89–90, 91–92

scaffolding and, 98–101

tips on, 97–98

VPT and, 19, 29*f,* 90–97

worksheet on, 103

writing concepts domain

charts for, 29*f,* 156, 158, 161

as early literacy component, 10, 17–18*f*

name writing and, 90, 92–94, 99–100

playing and, 79, 83

reading and, 53–54

singing and, 67–68

talking and, 39

VPT and, 19, 29*f,* 90–97, 156, 158, 161

Z

zipper songs, 70

zone of proximal development, 83